Once Upon a Bottom Line

Harnessing the Power of Storytelling in Sales

Sheryl Green

DEDICATION

To the memory of Mr. Robert Cawley, my first writing instructor. Your teaching helped me through one of the most difficult times in my life and continues to inspire me on a daily basis.

CONTENTS

Introduction

Conclusion

SHERYL GREEN

ACKNOWLEDGMENTS

Writing a book is truly a collaborative effort. I couldn't have done this without all of the experts that have come before me, the sales professionals who provided input, the storytellers that inspired me, the beta-readers and editor who provided feedback, my mentors who encouraged me and the friends and family that provided cute animal pictures and kind words when I was banging my head on the keyboard.

I'm sure that I'm missing people from this list (if I am, just blame the headache I got from the keyboard). Thank you to my amazing parents for all of the emotional support along the way; my awesome editor, Taryn Wittenwiler for fixing my grammatical atrocities; my beta-readers Mike Davis and Michael Wilson, Darren LaCroix for the swift kick in the butt; Melanie Rose for always taking the best pictures; Michelle Tyler for the beautiful cover; Clay Waldhalm for the constant stream of puppy videos; George Gilbert and Kathi Kulesza for talking me off the ledge more than once; Jessica Cline for the extra set of eyes during the outlining process; and John Polish, Maureen Zappala and Richard Warren for the many pieces of publishing guidance. Finally, thank you to Joe Wittenwiler —my brother from another mother — for believing in me even when I don't believe in myself.

INTRODUCTION

Thanks for picking up this book, and a big thanks for actually reading the introduction. I promise there's some good stuff in here that will set up the book for you and make this a pleasant and useful experience.

Before I get into what this book is about and how it can help you, I want to give you a little bit of background on me and why I decided to write it.

I was born in Oceanside, New York to... okay, maybe not that much background.

While most of my early working history was devoted to customer service positions, many of them also required that I sell products or services to the customers under the guise of "customer service." I have never wanted to be a salesperson (though I've since learned that it's inescapable), and frankly, I wasn't very good at it.

During college, I worked as a customer service representative at a bank and was tasked with selling checking and savings accounts, CDs, and the like. It was mind-numbing. I didn't want to appear pushy, but the company's "sell or die" attitude forced its employees to hawk unnecessary products to uneducated consumers. We were taught to lead with the features of the account, the interest rate, the lack of fees, the ease with which they could access their money, but we weren't actually solving a problem.

The experience left a bad taste in my mouth and caused a negative attitude towards "sales" that would last for almost two decades and span three states.

I left my husband and moved out to Las Vegas in 2008 (I promise, there's a reason I'm telling you this). As just about every woman does when she gets a divorce, I read Eat, Pray, Love by Elizabeth Gilbert. I'm not sure what men do after a divorce... football? Poker? Anyway, Gilbert talks about "divorced women classes" in her book. Apparently, when you get divorced, you have to sign up for classes at the community college and learn something. I had a lot of time on my hands and figured that taking a class could help me meet some new friends (not that I don't love my parents, but I needed to meet some people my own age).

I flipped through the College of Southern Nevada Continuing Education catalog, skipping over the foreign languages and accounting basics, until I found a writing class. I loved writing. I hadn't done it in a while, but had fond memories of the stories I used to write as a student in grade school. Enough time had passed since I'd had to write a paper, that I was no longer haunted by MLA and APA demons (the writing formats that you have to use in college... and they are painful).

I bought myself a nice, shiny notebook and headed into class the first day full of excitement.

Well, apparently these weren't just divorced women classes. They attracted the... umm... retired set. I was the youngest person in the class by about forty years. I was beginning to think that perhaps, I'd be better off learning Spanish, when our instructor walked in. Retired author and teacher, Mr. Robert Cawley. What he lacked in hearing ability, he made up for in encouragement. He was kind, knowledgeable, and had a lifetime of books under his belt.

Mr. Cawley stepped into the classroom, placed his things on the front table and smiled at this motley group of intrepid writers.

"We are storytellers," he said. "So let's tell a story."

For the next three months, Mr. Cawley opened class with the same line before instructing us to write an impromptu story in our notebooks.

You're probably wondering what this has to do with sales. At that time... nothing. But eight years later, it became really freaking important.

While I used writing as a cathartic outlet during my divorce, I needed more. I needed a support system and a purpose in life. I found these in animal rescue. I started out with a yard sale, raising over $1,000 for a brand-new rescue. I began doing adoption events, chatting with potential adopters and supervising playtime with available dogs and cats. There are so many stories here, but I'll save them for later (or the next book). Suffice it to say, within a few years of volunteering, I'd found the organization that felt like home, the volunteers that felt like family, and the animals to whom I would lend my voice and my energy to help protect. 400 pounds of dog fur in my car at all times was just a bonus.

I began organizing meetings with local business owners, wealthy individuals in the community, and foundations so I could raise money for our life-saving programs. I was back to doing sales. Only this time, I didn't have a product to sell.

Yup, if you've ever done non-profit work, you understand. You literally sit across from a potential donor and ask them to give you money when you have no product or service to give them in return. Sure, you're providing a safe haven for furry creatures (or whatever population you serve), improving the community in which you live, and giving that population the promise of a better future. But, let's be honest. Have you ever gone to the mall for a pair of shoes and some community improvement? I know I haven't.

Conventional sales wisdom tells you to forego the *features* of your product, and instead sell the *benefits* your product will provide to your customer. But what do you do when the *benefits* of your "product" won't be for the customer?

You sell emotion.

On my first real "fundraising meeting," I sat across the table from a potential donor. I could feel the sweat forming rivulets down my back as I threw every fact and figure I could think of at this guy. I explained how many animals were being killed in our shelters because there weren't enough homes for all of them. I told him how much it costs to spring an animal from the kill-shelter, provide food, medical attention, and a foster home for them until they could be adopted. I even told him how much it would cost to implement a community spay-and-neuter program so we could snip this problem in the bud and stop chasing our tails (every possible pun intended).

His eyes were glazed over. He kept looking past me to see if someone would come into the office and save him. He was checking his watch repeatedly and I was pretty sure he'd bolt at the first opportunity.

I was losing his attention. Worse, I was losing the possibility of saving more animals. I felt like a failure.

It was time to shift gears: numbers weren't working, the "features" of what the organization did weren't working, even the benefits to the community weren't peaking his interest. I was out of ideas. I just knew that I couldn't give up.

Then I heard Mr. Cawley's voice inside my head. (I did

promise that I was going somewhere with that.)

"We are storytellers... so let's tell a story."

A light bulb went off in my brain.

I quickly scrolled through my mental Rolodex for the perfect rescue story...

Gemma.

Yes! Gemma was this tiny Daschund mix who was dumped in the night drop at the local animal shelter. This is where they put the animals that have passed and are awaiting *disposal*. Shelter workers found her in the morning and brought her in to see the veterinarian. He examined little Gemma and discovered that while she appeared to be in good health, her back legs were paralyzed and nothing could be done for her. He decided that since there were so many "perfectly good" animals waiting for forever homes, Gemma would never make it to a permanent family.

This poor pup was sitting on the metal table as the veterinarian prepped the needle that would end her story, when one of our volunteers happened to be walking past the exam room. Gemma caught her eye through the small glass window.

Our volunteer barged into the room, scooped Gemma up off the table and brought her to our rescue where she was surrounded by a team of professional "aunties" who loved and snuggled her. We got a wheelchair donated for her so she could run with her front legs and roll her back legs behind her. Then she went into foster care with our Executive Director, Kelly, whose house is already set up to support disabilities.

While in foster care, Gemma received traditional and alternative medical treatments and just a few weeks after she was almost put down, she hopped off the couch and ran into Kelly's kitchen for dinner — without her wheelchair. I can safely say that each of the volunteers who received the video clip of Gemma running for the first time, can tell you exactly where they were, and exactly how much they cried (P.S. It was a lot).

Now Gemma has a wonderful daddy, furry siblings to play with, and an in-ground swimming pool, because apparently she is the doggy version of Michael Phelps.

I told my potential donor Gemma's story. I explained that it was because of generous contributions from community members just like him, that we were able to save Gemma and hundreds of other dogs and cats just like her.

And *that* is when the checkbook came out.

It's rarely enough to sell features. Sometimes, you can't even sell benefits. But what you can sell, are emotions. The way to do this, is through story.

I've been studying writing and the art of storytelling for approximately ten years now, though one could argue that I've been practicing my whole life. I've written three novels that are collecting dust on my hard drive. I've written and published a personal development book, and for the past five years, I've been working with businesses to tell their stories through website content, blogging, e-books, and more. I've studied under some of the greatest storytellers of our time, The Moth (a non-profit dedicated to the art and craft of storytelling) teacher Peter Aguero, speaker Craig Valentine, and Screenplay Consultant Michael Hague who works with Will Smith (yes, THE Will Smith). And of course, I can't forget Mr. Cawley.

How to Use this Book

The book is divided up into 3 different sections:

- Why you need stories in your business
- How to craft your stories
- Where to use them

My suggestion is to read it all the way through, and then go back and use it for reference while you are creating your own stories.

This book is not designed to help you become the next Hemingway or write the Great American Novel. There are plenty of other books out there if you want to become a bestselling author and tell fanciful tales of mystery and intrigue. Just as there are differences between a written story and an oral telling, there are also differences between telling a story for pure entertainment and telling a story to entice your audience to buy, donate, or otherwise participate in your world. This book is designed for those who want to improve the emotional connection they have with their audience so they can better meet the needs of that audience. I've created some helpful infographics for you to really drive home a few points. To download them, please head over to www.onceuponabottomline.com and click on Get the Graphics at the bottom of the page.

Be forewarned, I am a smartass. If you aren't chuckling while reading this book, I have failed and will hang my head in shame and offer myself up as a sacrifice to the gods of story. Storytelling should be powerful. It should be inspiring and persuasive. Most importantly, it should be fun. Because if we aren't having fun in life... well, then why are we here?

Part 1

Why You Need Stories in Your Business

CHAPTER ONE
IT'S NOT ABOUT THE TOILET PAPER

Do you remember when you were a little kid?

You'd get ready to go to sleep, dressed in your favorite superhero pajamas, snuggling into bed and pulling the covers up to your nose. Then, you'd wait for your parents to come in and read you some... statistics.

Wait, that's not right.

Nope, you were waiting for a bedtime story weren't you? You wanted to explore the department store with Corduroy as he searched for his missing button. You wanted to feel the tiny pea creating a lump in the bed that kept the princess up all night. You wanted to sail to an island where you'd be crowned king of the Wild Things, or listen as the Lorax spoke for the trees.

You, my friend, are wired for story. We all are. From the

moment we are born, no scratch that, from the moment we are conceived, we are trained to respond to story. From the first story read to your mom's belly, to the stories that will be told at your funeral, you are a creature of story. This is how we learn lessons, internalize societal mores, emotionally connect with other human beings, and influence behaviors.

In The Strategic Storyteller, Alexander Jutkowitz (2017) says, "Communication allows us to feel connected and helps us better understand ourselves, which is why storytelling has been an inherent, universal part of the human experience."

What does any of this have to do with sales?

Let me repeat the last two benefits of stories:

- Connect with other human beings
- Influence behaviors

That sounds a lot like the basics of sales. You need to connect with other human beings (your clients) in order to influence behaviors (get them to buy).

When you stand in the store comparing... let's say toilet paper... you think you are making a conscious decision based on price and quality. You think that you have intellectually weighed the pros and cons of each brand, carefully determining which product will work best for your family and your budget.

Wrong.

According to Gerald Zaltman, a professor at Harvard Business School, 95% of our purchase decision making takes place in the subconscious mind. Let me repeat that just in case you were daydreaming. 95% of our purchase decision making takes place in the subconscious mind. So, while you may think that you know what you're doing, you're actually being driven by a part of your brain that you have little to no control over.

Aargh! Why can't I just focus on buying toilet paper?

In "90 Percent of All Purchasing Decisions are Made Subconciously" Martin Lindstrom quotes behavioral economist George Loewenstein, "A major part of our brain is busy with automatic processes, not conscious thinking. A lot of emotions and less cognitive activities happen. Our brains usually run on autopilot, despite making us believe we know what we are doing. Thus, our subconscious explains our consumer behavior better than our conscious."

So, while you are staring at the price sticker, your brain is actually thinking, "but this one has a cute bear on it." It's not the cute bear that's swaying you (although that would probably be enough for me), it's actually the emotional attachment you have to the bear. You've been following the family through their toilet paper tribulations as they do what they do in the woods, and you are unknowingly rooting for them to enjoy a clean existence.

In All Marketers are Liars, Seth Godin (2012) suggests that,

"Consumers pretend that they're rational and careful and thoughtful about the stuff they buy. Actually, they're not. Instead, they rely on stories. Stories matter."

In fact, people don't even necessarily buy what they need. They buy what they want. Sure, everyone needs toilet paper — I just wrote a social media post about how everyone poops — but you have hundreds of options regarding what brand to buy. Which means that when it comes down to it, you buy the story you want to buy, not the actual toilet paper.

Godin says, "Needs are practical and objective, wants are irrational and subjective. And no matter what you sell and whether you sell it to businesses or consumers—the path to profitable growth is in satisfying wants, not needs. (Of course, your product must really satisfy those wants, not just pretend to!)."

This explains why you can buy a pair of basketball shoes (which you need if you play basketball) for $50, or you can buy them for $250 or $550. Are the latter any better? Probably not, but they come with a story. A story about how much better you will become at basketball by wearing them.

Are you ready for something cool?

In 2009, Rob Walker and Joshua Glenn devised a "literary and anthropological experiment" to prove the hypothesis "Narrative transforms insignificant objects into significant ones." They also set out to demonstrate that, not only can story increase the subjective value of an object, but it can also be measured objectively. They visited yard sales, flea markets, and thrift stores looking for tchotchkes. They purchased items for around $1.25 a piece and then paired participating writers with each object. The writers created a fictional story (with no intention of fooling the customer) for their item and then posted it on eBay. The results? $128.74 worth of junk was sold for $3,612.51. That's an ROI (Return On Investment) of 27.06%. Not too shabby. Turns out this storytelling thing might be something to pay attention to. In case you're wondering, the proceeds from the study went to the writers and to non-profits that support mentoring and tutoring. You can read more about the study and the stories at www.significantobjects.com.

There's an old adage in the writing world, "Don't tell me, show me."

Stories allow us to do just that. Don't tell your customers that you can help them. Show them how you've helped other people in their situation. Harness the power of story to show your potential clients exactly what you do, how you do it (and by this I mean with integrity, good customer service, and whatever else matters to you), and how you can fix their problem.

I've been doing sales for years and I'm doing just fine.

That's cool. But could you be doing better?

Your customers like you. They buy from you. Occasionally, they even send referrals your way. Life is good. But could it be better?

Arianna Huffington talks about storytelling in her book Thrive (2014). She says:

> Humans are hardwired for narrative; we may be the only creatures who see our own lives as part of a larger narrative. Though we're told by physicists that time doesn't exist as we think it does, we're still very much creatures of time. And time inherently creates a story. Jung called the universal language of stories 'archetypes.' He described them as 'ancient river beds along which our psychic current naturally flows.' Our conscious minds relate to these archetypes through stories. Far from simply serving as entertainment or diversion, stories are a universal language about the purpose of life itself.

Business is constantly changing and competition is getting stiffer every day. Between the countless companies popping up each year and the influx of Internet-based businesses to the market, it's getting more and more difficult to get (and keep) the attention of your potential buyers.

If you've been doing "just fine" with your sales, it may be because you have a unique product. It may be because your buyers already know that they need what you have.

All of that could change in an instant.

Picking up this book is the first step in staying ahead of the competition. Learn (and master) the art of storytelling before the market goes flooky (new word, feel free to use it), and watch your business grow. Storytelling may just be the most important skill you ever learn.

If you haven't read the Introduction, please go back and check it out. I'm going to refer back to the stories in there throughout the book and you are going to be as lost as Hansel and Gretel in the forest if you don't read the Introduction first. I can wait a few minutes.

Welcome back! Now that you know who I am and why I'm telling you all of this, we can move on.

CHAPTER 2
YOUR BRAIN ON STORY

Do you remember those PSAs in the 80's from the Partnership for a Drug-Free America? There was a frying pan on the stove with some butter in it (that's drugs), then they'd add an egg (your brain) to the mix and it would become a sizzling mess. Well, that was your brain on drugs. *This* is your brain on story. (And it's much prettier)

I'm going to throw some science-y terms out right now so hold on to your pocket protectors.

As you probably know, there are a variety of hormones created by the human body that act as neurotransmitters, which create different responses when they are released. The important hormones to focus on right now are: Cortisol, Oxytocin, and Dopamine. Let's take a closer look at what each one does and then we'll discuss why we care.

Cortisol is known as the stress hormone, or the "fight or flight" hormone. I wish you could donate cortisol like you donate blood... I'd be a millionaire. Anyway, it's perfectly normal to produce cortisol and it actually does a lot of good, like regulating metabolism, controlling blood pressure, reducing inflammation, and keeping your body's salt and water in balance. All of that is lovely, but the benefit we really care about is how it improves focus.

Oxytocin, on the other hand, is sometimes referred to as the trust hormone. Neuroeconomist Paul Zak, calls it the "it's safe to approach others" signal in the brain. This hormone enhances our sense of empathy and our ability to experience others' emotions. "Why Your Brain Loves Good Storytelling "

Finally, Dopamine is released by our brain's reward center: the limbic system. It makes us feel optimistic and reduces depression.

So, why did I just give you a biology lesson? Because Paul Zak's research found that storytelling evokes a strong neurological response.

First: Character-driven stories release oxytocin, causing us to empathize with the characters, putting ourselves in their shoes and cheering them on.

Second: When presented with the challenge or stressor in a story, our bodies produce cortisol which helps us focus in on the story.

Third: When the story has a happy ending, it releases dopamine and we are left feeling hopeful about the future.

As a salesperson or marketer, would it behoove you to have potential customers empathize with a character of your choosing, feel that character's stress as the challenges are presented, and then feel relief and pleasure when the problem is solved (with your product or service)?

There's this little game that's played once a year. I believe they call it the "Super Bowl." Have you heard of it? Well, a 30-second commercial spot costs around $4 million. Pocket change, of course.

Anyway, when you're dropping $4 million dollars for 30 seconds, you've got to create gold... or platinum. Keith A. Quesenberry is a researcher at Johns Hopkins University and after conducting a 2-year analysis of 108 Super Bowl commercials, he found that commercials with dramatic plotlines rated much higher among viewers than those without.

According to Quesenberry in the article "Super Bowl Ads," "People think it's all about sex or humor or animals, but what we've found is that the underbelly of a great commercial is whether it tells a story or not."

Now if you'll excuse me for a moment, I'm off to watch the commercial that has it all: Budweiser Clydesdale Puppy Love Super Bowl 2014 Commercial.

OMG. I'm not going to lie. I just cried. Clearly, they nailed the "evoking emotion" part of storytelling. And if I drank beer, I'd for sure try Budweiser.

As humans, we relate to emotions, not to experience. I've never been best friends with a horse (though I'm totally open to it if you know one), but I have been sad when I've lost someone.

So what are the emotions that we should be shooting for?

Well, that's changed a bit in the last few years. It was previously believed that there were six basic human emotions: happiness, sadness, fear, anger, surprise, and disgust. Then researchers at Glasgow University used cameras to take 3-dimensional images of people who were trained to activate all 42 individual facial muscles independently (Think: Jim Carey). Based on their findings, there are only four basic emotions: happy, sad, afraid/surprised, and angry/disgusted. "How Many Basic Emotions are There? Fewer Than Previously Thought"

I'd spend some time arguing that I'd be "surprised" if my dog brought me breakfast in bed, but I certainly wouldn't classify myself as "afraid" under those circumstances — unless of course she hadn't washed her paws before cooking — but it's a moot point since the science changed again.

Alan S. Cowen and Dacher Keltner, PhDs from the University of California, Berkeley, have now identified 27 categories of emotions:

- Admiration
- Adoration
- Aesthetic Appreciation
- Amusement
- Anxiety
- Awe
- Awkwardness
- Boredom
- Calmness
- Confusion
- Craving
- Disgust
- Empathetic pain
- Entrancement
- Envy
- Excitement
- Fear
- Horror
- Interest
- Joy
- Nostalgia
- Romance
- Sadness
- Satisfaction
- Sexual desire
- Sympathy
- Triumph

Do any of those sound familiar? Chances are that, every day, you experience several such emotions. If you're like me, you've probably had a day when you've blown through most of them. Whether there are six, four, twenty-seven, or one hundred (not yet, but who knows?) emotions, there are 7.6 billion humans occupying this planet as we speak. You may be worried that you won't be able to tap into the emotion of your potential customers, but I think it's safe to say the odds are stacked in your favor.

Stop and Smell the Stories

Now I'm not sure if you've noticed, but there's a lot of information out there. More is being added every day. We've gone from encyclopedias and card catalogs to the internet. I don't know much about how data is stored, but I don't think that we are going to run out of space for content anytime soon. This is great news for people (like me) who create content for a living. It's great for people (also like me) who love to learn and are constantly looking for more information. There's so much information out there, we could never possibly consume all of it. Even if we somehow did, there's no way that we could remember it all. But what can we remember? You guessed it. Stories.

Need some scientific proof? According to Lisa Cron, author of <u>Wired for Story</u> (2012): "In the second it takes you to read this sentence, your senses are showering you with over 11,000,000 pieces of information. Your conscious mind is capable of registering about forty of them. And when it comes to actually paying attention? On a good day, you can process seven bits of data at a time. On a bad day, five. On one of *those* days? More like minus three."

Oh yeah, I've had one of *those* days.

As living creatures, we all have one main goal: survival. We, along with all animals, were given instincts - that little voice inside of us that tells us not to touch a hot stove. But it didn't stop there. Humans got an extra way to navigate and process information... story. Make note: this is probably the only time in my life where I will say that humans are better than animals.

Need that spelled out? You're not likely to see mommy and daddy chipmunks sitting around a fire pit explaining to their baby chipmunks about the time Uncle Chippy got drunk at a party, ran through a campfire, and burned his tail fur off.

Cron quotes neuroscientist Antonio Damasio, "The problem of how to make all this wisdom understandable, transmissible, persuasive, enforceable — in a word, of how to make it stick- was faced and a solution found. Storytelling was the solution: storytelling is something brains do, naturally and implicitly.... it should be no surprise that it pervades the entire fabric of human societies and cultures."

This is your brain on story.

CHAPTER THREE
UGH, DO I REALLY HAVE TO DO THIS?

Yes. Yes, you do. There's so much selling power in stories. Don't you want to harness it? If not, it's like sitting in a dark room and refusing to turn on the lights.

There are three reasons that you must (must!) use story in your business and your sales:

- Emotion
- Brand
- Your customer demands it

"Even in our oversaturated, overcrowded media environment, there will always be room for another good story." - Strategic Storyteller

Let's take a closer look at these 3 reasons.

Emotion

A few months before I sat down to write this book, Las Vegas saw its most violent, senseless tragedy to date. On October 1st, gunshots rained down on concert-goers at the Route 91 festival. The shooter was holed up in a hotel room in the Mandalay Bay and managed to kill fifty-eight people and injure hundreds more before taking his own life. Even after the initial shock wore off, recounting the story still makes my hair follicles twitch and tears well up in my eyes.

The numbers were staggering, but it wasn't until names and pictures of the victims were released that the true horror of the experience hit. These were actual people. Husbands, wives, parents, children. Lives and families torn apart because of senseless violence.

As a tribute to the lives lost, a remembrance wall was built in downtown Las Vegas with names, pictures, and personal effects. Never liking to cry in public (now, I'm not saying I don't do it — I'm just saying I don't *like* to do it), I tried to keep a straight face. I could mourn for my city in private. Until I saw one of the tributes: 25 Years my Husband. Forever my hero.

Even now, I'm crying into my green tea. I didn't know this person. I still don't know which one of the victims it was meant for. All I know, is that when an emotional connection is forged, it can't be undone.

Emotion not only makes <u>you </u>vulnerable, it also gives others the freedom to be vulnerable, as well. When you tell them about your struggles and challenges, you provide the space for them to share theirs.

My clients often ask me: How much of my story should I share in a business setting?

I'm sure there are other experts out there who will argue that there's no place for personal stories in a business setting, but I don't agree. Your story, your experiences, have power. They have the power to connect, to unite, and to sell. This isn't carte blanche permission to air your dirty laundry while you're trying to sell... a washing machine. I used to work with a boss who thought that we all needed to hear about his sex life. I assure you, we did not. That wasn't sharing a story for a purpose. He just liked to talk about his sexcapades.

Anyway, your stories must always be true and relevant, and if they can help someone relate to your situation and find refuge in your product or service... share away.

When I was interviewing salespeople and fundraisers for this book, I sat down with my friend Caitlin who works with Junior Achievement.

When Caitlin told me about the Junior Achievement children going to school hungry, not having the ability to shower because they were living in a car, and the ones who were being abused, I became emotionally invested. Not because I have a huge soft spot for kids. If you know me, you know that while I don't dislike kids, my warm fuzzies are all saved up for animals. I was emotionally invested because I had a story of my own that I could relate to her organization's mission.

I used to substitute teach in the school district. I actually preferred the Resource Classrooms in elementary schools because they allowed me to work with a smaller group of children at a time, and I didn't have the responsibility of walking them to and from the bathroom, lunch, and specials (gym, library, etc.). Well, one day I had a kid steal a little toy from my classroom. It was probably worth 22 cents, but I felt that I needed to make a point so his behavior wouldn't continue outside the classroom.

I kneeled down and in my best talking-to-children voice said, "I know that you took something from my classroom. That didn't belong to you. How would you feel if someone took your things and you couldn't play with them anymore?"

The kid burst into tears. It wasn't unexpected. In the few years I spent in classrooms, I witnessed a lot of tears. But this kid was inconsolable.

Please keep in mind that I was usually in a different classroom, a different school altogether, every day. I didn't know any of these kids, I was just there to make sure no one lit anything on fire (which as you will read in Chapter 6, I once failed). I had no idea what any of these children were dealing with at home.

I found out.

When another teacher happened to walk by, she asked what was going on and I filled her in. She promptly handed the toy back to the kid and sent him to class. Once he was out of earshot, she informed me that his parents had abandoned him, he went from foster home to foster home, and all of his possessions could fit in a suitcase.

Oy vey.

Caitlin wasn't even trying to sell me as a supporter of the non-profit. It was completely inadvertent. That's the power of story to evoke emotion. Sometimes, you don't even mean to do it.

Maybe your audience isn't itching to tell you a story in return, but you can bet that they are relating your story to something that has happened or is happening in their lives at that moment.

In Lead with a Story, Smith (2012) tells a story of above and beyond customer service. You may want to grab a tissue for this one.

In a small town in Arkansas, there were no sandwich shops to be found. Sterling Price, an employee at Pizza Hut was approached by a woman asking for a meatball sub. Sterling apologized, as meatball subs weren't on the menu. At which point, the woman was on the verge of tears. Realizing that they had all of the ingredients he needed, Sterling agreed to make the meatball sub.

"She thanked me profusely, and then explained that her husband was very sick and had lost his appetite. She was desperate to get him to eat something, and had asked him if there was anything that sounded good. He told her he might be able to eat some of a meatball sandwich. She'd been to several restaurants already and no one could help her."

Pizza Hut was the last stop she was going to make before accepting defeat.

The woman returned the next day to thank Sterling and explained the situation further. "It turns out her husband had been diagnosed with stage four cancer a few months earlier. His loss of appetite was the least of his unpleasant symptoms, but perhaps the only one she could provide any comfort for."

Her husband had passed away during the night and that sandwich had been his last meal.

Now, when I first read this story, I was staying with my parents for a few weeks. My dad was recovering from a surgery, my stepmom was suffering from a broken rib and toes after a fall. I was cooking, cleaning, shopping, and picking up random dropped objects. Because I was going through a similar situation, the customer service story was touching. I felt for this woman caring for her husband and doing everything in her power to make his life a little easier. Not because I knew her, but because I could relate.

When used properly, stories transport us into the emotions of the hero, even if we can't see ourselves in their exact circumstances.

<u>Brand</u>

"In business, the right story defines any company's most valuable asset: it's brand." - Alexander Jutkowitz

Who are you?

This isn't some metaphysical question meant to make your brain go all twisty. It's a straightforward, who are you, what do you do, and why do you do it, question. It's something that you better be able to answer and then stick to, or you will confuse your current and potential customers and send them running to your closest competitor. The term "brand" has become so overused that (in my humble opinion) it's destined to join terms like "synergy" and "optimization" in the Business Hall of Shame. However, that doesn't make your brand any less important. Your brand communicates who you are to the world — it is the reputation that you must uphold — and your brand story is the foundation on which you build. In case you have no idea what I'm talking about right now, a brand story is a narrative about your business that is designed to evoke emotion. We'll discuss how to develop this story in a later chapter.

About two years ago, I visited a Toastmasters club that was

in my area when I served as Area Director. The woman I had groomed to replace me, gave me a big hug and said, "I check your feed every morning. You've developed quite a brand on Facebook."

I remember thanking her, all the while thinking, "I'm developing a brand on Facebook?"

Let's play a little game. I want you to open your favorite social media feed and look through your posts. Wait! Don't go yet. You're just looking at *your* posts. I don't want you to get sucked into the neverland of social media never to be seen again. Okay, go.

How many of those posts were negative? How many were complaining about the minute details of life? Do you take pictures of all of your food? Does every fourth picture have an adoptable animal (ahem ahem)? Is it selfie after selfie with the dreaded duck face? Who are you and what are you communicating to your followers?

Like it or not (and purposefully or not), you tell your brand story with every single post.

Just yesterday, I was about to rant on Facebook about how when I'm stressed (which is about as common as a penguin being one bowtie away from formal attire), I tend to organize and purge any personal belongings that I haven't used in the last twelve minutes. Such purging makes Halloween costumes difficult, but I'm used to that. What I'm not used to, is the feeling of horror from having thrown something useful away. (Why would I donate a podcasting microphone?!?)

I had the post typed out, all ready to go. Then I realized that I'm not a negative Nancy. Stressed as I may be at times, I keep my posts inspirational, uplifting, funny, and filled with furry friends awaiting their forever homes. I deleted my post, texted a friend my dilemma, and then moved on with my life.

Story is powerful and necessary, but if you don't uphold what it is you want people to know about you, your brand will crumble in a little heap of inauthenticity.

Remember, your actions can either bolster or undermine your words.

I'm proud to say that wasn't even a quote. That was my brilliance shining through. You're welcome.

Anyway, imagine if I spent my days touting the benefits of pet adoption, educating my followers on cruelty in the cosmetics industry, posting pictures of available cuties, and asking for donations for my rescue. Well, you don't have to imagine that part... that happens. Now imagine that after a long day of all of the above, I head out to a nightclub wearing a Cruella-esque coat made of Golden Retriever tails.

How will you feel the next day when I ask for donations to my rescue?

Once you've crafted that brand story, stick to it. Seth Godin says, "When you find a story that works, live that story, make it true, authentic, and subject to scrutiny."

Sheryl, I don't think I need a brand story.

"The world will ask you who you are, and if you don't know, the world will tell you," said Carl Jung.

Trust me, you need a story. What happens when you don't craft and share a brand story? Let's just say it's not pretty.

According to Jankowitz, "For anybody crafting a reputation, either for themselves or for a company, this is important to remember. Unless you make the raw ingredients of your big-picture story available, either to your friends and family, your potential customers, or the public in general, they'll use whatever they have to construct their own guiding narrative about you. Even without realizing it, people are always making up stories in their heads and casting elements of the world around them as characters. It's something that's going to happen with or without your input."

I guess the question at this point, is whether or not you'd like to create your own identity, or have it created for you.

The Customer Demands It

Do you remember the fable The Emperor's New Clothes by Hans Christian Anderson? Don't worry if you don't, I'm about to give you a recap that will likely have dear ol' Hans rolling in his grave.

There was once a king whose priorities were a tad bit wonky. I suppose one could call him vain, as his biggest concern was wearing the latest fashion and showing it off to his subjects. One day, two con artists rode into town with a promise of the finest fabric. Not only would their outfit be the best ever, it would also appear invisible to "fools," giving the king the opportunity to weed through his people and see the quality of the company he kept.

 (But really, they were weaving nothing and the king was about to be... chilly.)

I just want to hop out of the story for one moment and ask, "What did the king think these 'fools' would see if they didn't see his clothes?"

Back to the story. The king was all over this idea and paid the con artists a ton of money for his new clothes. But when he went to see the clothing items... he couldn't. Afraid of being labeled a fool, he sent his most respected advisor to check on the progress. That guy couldn't see them either. Long story short, no one wanted to admit that they couldn't see anything (as it would've meant they were fools), so instead, the king walked around buck naked for a few hours just to prove that he wasn't a fool.

Now, I'm not calling all consumers fools (although I can think of plenty of purchases that might fit into the "new clothes" category), I'm just suggesting that people don't mind being lied to as long as they get to play along with the lie and derive some benefit from it. In fact, they actually demand the lie.

We see this constantly in the marketing world, and I'm only mildly ashamed to say that I fall victim to it as well. How? Well, I think you've ascertained throughout this book that I'm a bit of an animal lover. Would it surprise (or disappoint you) to know that I'm also an omnivore? I'd love to tell you that I'm a hardcore vegan and nothing I eat has ever hurt, nor even offended, an animal.

But that would be a lie. My body doesn't do well without animal protein. However, one of my life goals is to be able to afford to only eat Wagyu beef. Why? Because I've been told a great story and I choose to play along. Wagyu cows roam free in a beautiful countryside, they are given beer, and they receive daily massages. Yes, they still die; however, in my mind, if I get a massage and an alcoholic treat every day for a year or so, you can eat me. (Dear serial killers, I'm just trying to make a point here. Please do not see this as an invitation. Thank you.)

I like this story and takes away some of my guilt for having to eat another animal to survive.

When you walk into a real estate open house, you'll likely smell fresh-baked cookies. Everyone knows that this is a sales technique to trick potential buyers into feeling like this could be a nice "home" not just a house. (Wait, everyone knows that, right? I hope I'm not going to be attacked by an angry mob of realtors.) Anyway, we know the trick, but that doesn't make us any less susceptible to it. We want to believe that we are going to have a happy life filled with fun, laughter, and slightly under-baked snicker doodles. Yum. We want to believe, so we play along.

This storytelling only becomes a problem when the company or marketer is up to no good. While I was working at that bank in college, I had a customer come to see me in tears. She was an elderly woman who had seen a commercial for a mortgage product on television. The spokesperson was a retired baseball great. She explained that when she saw him on television, she instantly trusted the company. After all, he was "a good Italian boy from Brooklyn." Unfortunately, he was also a paid spokesperson. And he was paid from the profit of the sketchy loans they offered to vulnerable old people. She wanted to believe the story. Unfortunately, it bit her in the butt.

According to Godin, "Stories let us lie to ourselves. And those lies satisfy our desires. It's the story, not the good or service you actually sell, that pleases the consumer."

There's another aspect to the customers' demand for stories: what they will and will not tolerate.

A few years ago, I worked in a mental health facility. As a Day Treatment Counselor for the severely mentally ill, my job was to talk to the clients, not from a medically therapeutic standpoint (that was out of my "scope" of practice), but more from a big sister mentality. I'll be honest... I wasn't very good at it. My officemate on the other hand, was fantastic. He always had a line of clients waiting to talk to him because he was kind, non-judgmental, and most importantly, he understood how to talk to them. Not the words (though he had that down, too), but rather, his body language. You see, he would sit down *next* to the clients rather than across from them. He would turn his head to look at them, but it was always from the side. I asked him once why he did that and he said, "It's less confrontational. These people are used to everyone telling them what to do from a position of authority. They appreciate that I bring myself to their level and don't tell them what they *have* to do, but rather give them practical suggestions so they can make a decision on their own."

Great advice for those who interact with the mentally ill on a regular basis, but also a good technique for those who want to provide services or products to someone. You know what they need. You know that your product would cure what ails them. But if you approach them in a confrontational "You have to do this" manner... it's not going to go very well.

One more example: I occasionally cover for a friend of mine who pet sits. I enjoy snuggling the furry little monsters so I'm happy to step up when she goes on vacation. I took a job for her last month, two kitties owned by a very well-to-do woman. A woman who called me up at 7 am on Saturday (I didn't start the job till Sunday) to tell me: "You have to go to my house and pick up my clothes and then overnight them to me."

Ummm... excusez moi?

Let the record reflect that I will give you the shirt off my back (but not right now because it's cold!), as long as you ask nicely. I have no problem helping people or going out of my way to serve a client, but I don't take kindly to being told what I *have* to do.

Are you doing that to your customers? Are you barking orders at them, or are you illustrating how your product could help them? Chip and Dan Heath talk about the power of storytelling in their book Made to Stick (2007). In it, they tell the story of Stephen Denning who worked for the World Bank. Denning learned that "springboard stories" (stories that let people see how an existing problem might change) were not ambiguous, peripheral, or anecdotal, as he once thought.

> Why not spell out the message directly? Why go to the trouble of trying to elicit the listener's thinking indirectly, when it would be so much simpler if I come straight out in an abstract directive? Why not hit the listener between the eyes? The problem is, that when you hit listeners between the eyes they respond by fighting back. The way you deliver a message to them is cue to how they should react. If you make an argument, you're implicitly asking them to evaluate your argument - judge it, debate it, criticize it- and then argue back, at least in their minds. But with a story, Denning argues, you engage the audience - you are involving people with the idea, asking them to participate with you.

Potential customers or clients don't want to be blatantly told: "You need my product." Think about a time you've been confronted with a hard sell like this. Did you exclaim "Oh my God! You're so right! I've been waiting for this product my whole life!" or did you grab for your cell phone, which clearly didn't ring, and say "I have to take this," before making a beeline for the nearest exit?

You catch more dogs with a Kong full of peanut butter than with a shock collar.

Why use the power of story? Because it creates an emotional connection with your audience, creates and reinforces your brand, and because your customer demands it. So I guess the real question is: why *wouldn't* you use the power of story?

*** I promise, no Golden Retrievers were hurt during the making of this book.

CHAPTER FOUR
NOT ANOTHER STARFISH: WHAT STORY IS... AND ISN'T

Before we get much further, it's important to discuss the differences between fiction and non-fiction. You may have been lead to believe that fiction is the only place where you will encounter stories, characters, and dialogue, whereas non-fiction is a black abyss of information, statistics, data, facts, etc.

This is not true! Continuing to believe this will hamper your ability to tell stories for business. The only difference between the two is that one is true and one is made up. I've always used the mnemonic device of:

Fiction is Fake
Non-Fiction is Not Fake

When you are telling stories for your business, you will be

working in the realm of non-fiction most of the time. This doesn't mean that you will not use stories, just that you will not often make them up. Now, you may, every once in a while make up a story. This will not cause the world to end. Unless you don't tell your customer that you are making it up. We'll get into this later. For now, let's just assume that you will only be telling true (non-fictional) stories to your customers.

Let's address anecdotes quickly so we don't have to backtrack. In <u>Business Storytelling for Dummies</u>, Dietz and Silverman define an anecdote as: "A short personal account (your personal take on a situation). It tends to leave out sensory information and dialogue as well as context and setting." Think about it as a more factual and less entertaining, flowing narrative.

So what exactly is a story for business?

According to Handley (<u>Everybody Writes</u>), "Storytelling as it applies to business isn't about spinning a yarn or fairytale. Rather, it's about how your business (or its products and services) exist in the real world: who you are and what you do for the benefit of others, and how you add value to people's lives, ease their troubles, help shoulder their burdens, and meet their needs."

Cover the ears of your inner-rebel, please.

There are some rules that you need to follow in order to create these stories and take your audience on a journey. Let's start with a list and then we'll flesh each one out.

- It must be True (unless you tell them up front that it's not)
- It must be Original
- It must be Simple
- It must be Human (even if it doesn't include people)
- It must Serve the Customer
- It must be a Part of a Bigger Plan

Got that? Good. In we dive.

Rule # 1: True

This rule is my absolute favorite. Why? Because I didn't even think of it until I read <u>All Marketers are Liars</u>. That's right, the thought that someone would try to pass off a made up story as their own didn't even enter into my mind. That means that I'm either incredibly honest or incredibly naive. Take your pick.

According to Seth Godin (2012), "Just because people may believe your story, doesn't give you a right to tell it." This goes beyond the common courtesy of not feeding your audience a crap sandwich; untrue stories could actually cause physical harm.

Apparently, decades ago, Nestle decided that their sales were more important than the health of more than a million babies. They told a story about how much better baby formula was over breastfeeding. Unfortunately, too many consumers believed this story. Moms made the switch to powdered formula, often diluting it to save money, and occasionally using unclean water. The babies suffered.

This being said, if you plan to use the power of storytelling for anything other than good, if you plan to deceive, swindle, or hoodwink your audience... this isn't the book for you.

If you are still reading, you are an upstanding citizen and want to use story to help your customers embrace the solutions that they need to solve their problems. Consider this book the Hitch of the sales world. I just want to help you get out of your own way so you can bring your audience what they need.

Godin talks about two different questions that the consumer can ask the marketer to determine the authenticity of the marketing stories and claims. We will go into profiling your audience in a later chapter, for now, I just want you to put yourself in their shoes and ask:

1) If I knew what you know, would I choose to buy what you sell?

2) After I've used this and experienced it, will I be glad I believed the story or will I feel ripped off?

I think there's an even easier way to determine your authenticity... are you a customer of your own company?

Yup, it's that simple. If you are a snake oil salesman touting the benefit of your brew for everything from male pattern baldness to an inability to swing dance, yet you either don't drink your own cocktail or you are wearing a toupee and have two left feet... chances are you're lying.

I'm a firm believer in CBD oil and have sold it in the past. I was comfortable doing so because I was also a customer. I'd watched my stepmom go from a full slate of medications cooked up in a lab that had side effects more severe than her Rheumatoid Arthritis, to a daily dose of CBD oil, which kept her flare-ups under control and didn't destroy her immune system. With CBD oil, I was able to go off anti-anxiety medications and no longer had problems with an old boxing injury to my left wrist (I assure you that sounds way cooler than it actually was). If you know something works, and you have the personal evidence to back it up, there won't be any question that you are telling the truth.

If you decide to betray your audience's trust, and you get caught... Ouch. It's nearly impossible to ever get that trust back.

There is, of course, one caveat to this rule. If you are very obviously telling a fictional story (it's either so obvious it doesn't require announcing, or you let the audience know ahead of time), it doesn't have to be true.

I'm going to jump to the next rule and then we'll backtrack because I've got a doozy of an example that applies to both rules.

Rule # 2: Original

You've probably heard the term USP, or Unique Selling

Proposition, thrown around like a hacky sack at a Grateful Dead concert. It's constantly airborne because it's super important. Both you (your company) and your story must be unique. What is it that makes you special? What separates you from your competitors and helps you stand out and be heard above the roar of the crowd?

If you don't know this, your potential customers won't either.

This is the first question that I ask my clients when we sit down to work on their website content. "What makes you special?"

This is the time for horn tooting. This is not the time to sit back and be modest. When we get started with the interview process, I'll get answers like "I'm honest and reliable" or "I'm transparent" or my favorite one "I put customers first."

Groan.

First of all, I hate the word "transparent." It makes me think of the Visible Man toy I had growing up. It had clear, plastic "skin" that allowed you to see the skeletal system, organs, blood vessels, etc. If you are not clear, please don't use the word "transparent". If you are clear, please go to the doctor; something may be wrong with you.

Now let's destroy "honest", "reliable", and "I put customers first".

Ummm... of course you are and of course you do. That's called being a good business person. If you are currently swimming (or drowning) in the online dating pool, or have been recently, this is akin to a man saying "I have a steady job, a car of my own, and I no longer live in my parent's basement."

Well whoop-de-doo! You are a functioning adult. Don't parade that around. That's the bare minimum. So is putting your customers first.

I want to know what's different about YOU.

And when you tell me a story, I don't want it to be one that I've heard somewhere else... or that I've seen on a pillow in a greeting card store.

A few months ago, I happened to wander by a speaking engagement at the World Market Furniture Center. The speaker was discussing a very controversial topic (I'll spare the details to protect the guilty), which I would bet could have been told with any of a MILLION stories. Instead, he chose to tell the story of the starfish. You know the one, it's probably on a thank you card somewhere in your house right now.

Here's the gist, in case you've been living under a rock for the last decade.

Little girl on the beach throwing starfish back into the water.

Man walks by and asks why. She can't possibly save all of the starfish. She can't make a difference.

Girl tosses another starfish in and says, "I made a difference to that one."

Queue the "oohs" and "awws."

I promptly called my friend/speech-writing coach and said, "He told the starfish story!" And we had a nice ol' groanfest together.

Do. Not. Tell the starfish story (or any derivation specific to your industry). Everyone has heard it and it's not personal. If you take a good look at your career, your life, or the world around you, you are bound to find a story that you can share. We'll discuss where to mine for gold later on in the book.

I had an experience just a few weeks ago that I think pertains to both Rule # 1 and Rule # 2.

A client hired me to write a blog introducing another speaker that he was collaborating with. I had to do some research into the speaker's world, and then create the blog. So I did my due diligence, picking blogs and articles at random to get a feel for this person.

I found one about how he had been a loyal customer of one car rental company (which, for a speaker who travels most of their life, could put the car rental company onto the Forbes list and send every employee's child to Harvard.) He was a loyal customer until they didn't have a car for him and he had to go elsewhere. Well, when he arrived at the new rental company, he discovered that his license was expired (just by a day!) and they wouldn't rent him a car. Instead, they offered to drive him around to his different locations. Angels sang, the gods of customer service did pirouettes, and he is now a loyal customer of the new company.

This is a powerful story that shows how you must go above and beyond with your customers to create an experience that keeps them coming back for more.

There's just one problem. As I was researching for this book, I came across a great story about customer service. There was a car rental customer who's license had expired... do you see where I'm going with this?

I felt bamboozled and a tad bit dirty. Who was I to believe? Did this actually happen to anyone? Did this happen to both of them?

Now let me say that I am not accusing anyone of plagiarism or stealing stories, I'm simply pointing out the pitfalls if someone were to use someone else's experience as their own. Here I am, a potential customer, and I don't know who to believe. It makes me doubt the speaker's sincerity, their authenticity, and every single word that comes out of their mouth now.

Please don't do that to your potential customers. Give them something unique to you. Give them your experience, your take on something, or at least give them a heads up that you are going to share a story that isn't your own.

Rule # 3: Simple

What is the core message of your story?

Well, I want people to understand that they need my product, that they shouldn't go it alone, and that life is better when they buy what I'm selling... and that butterflies are pretty.

Yes, yes, butterflies are pretty but you only get one core message per story. If you try and communicate more than one core message, you'll lose your audience. The core message of this book is that you need to use stories to emotionally connect with your potential customers and increase your sales. Everything I do is in service of that core message. Breaking it down further, each individual story I share has one takeaway. One idea that you should learn and understand. More than that and you get nothing.

Chip and Dan Heath talk about this in <u>Made to Stick</u>. "To get to the core, we've got to weed out superfluous and tangential elements. But that's the easy part. The hard part is weeding out ideas that may be really important but just aren't the most important idea. The Army's Commander's Intent forces its officers to highlight the most important goal of an operation. The value of the Intent comes from its singularity. You can't have five North Stars, you can't have five "most important goals," and you can't have five Commander's Intents."

Every time you create a story, you must keep it simple, so that the most important core message is communicated, and so it can be shared.

Please allow me to be the harbinger of bad news for just a moment. This new fandangled social media craze that's sweeping the world... doesn't mean that you have access to everyone.

It's okay to sit down for a moment and fan yourself. I know you've been led to believe that the answer to your marketing woes is to get on the internet. And it's good, don't get me wrong. It may even be the best thing since sliced bread, but you still won't reach everyone.

What does this have to do with crafting a simple story? Let's just say that your ideal customer lives in a cabin in the middle of the woods. He doesn't have access to the internet, and he doesn't want it. What he does want is... hmm... what would he want? Oh! He wants a new ax to chop down the trees on his neighbor's property in the middle of the night (they've had a feud going for years). It just so happens that you have created an ax with a flashlight in the handle (if this doesn't exist, and you decide to create it after reading this book, please credit me in your story and then donate a portion of the proceeds to your local animal rescue).

There you are with the answer to his problems. But how will he know about it? He doesn't have a computer, a TV, or a newspaper subscription. His favorite carrier pigeon is on holiday in the South of France. All hope is lost.

But wait! He has a daughter. A daughter who delights in the pleasures of our modern, technologically advanced world and just happened to see your new light-up ax story on her Facebook feed this morning. Dad doesn't like her spending her money to buy him things, so she won't purchase it for him... but she can tell him about it.

Aha! We are finally there (I know it took awhile, but aren't you starting to feel a connection to our woodsy friend and his world-traveling bird?). If your story is simple, if it allows the audience to connect with your brand, it will be memorable. Daughter will now go visit her father and tell him about this light-up ax and why the company developed it. Mr. Woodsy now wants the ax and you just earned yourself a new customer that your marketing would never have reached in a million years.

The power of story in marketing is not rooted in you sharing your story with others... it's from them sharing your story with their circle.

I'll bring up this company later (because I LOVE them), but their story helps drive home the lesson here, as well. A few years ago, I went looking for the perfect, paper planner (say that 5 times fast). Yes, I'm analog and loving it. Anyway, I wanted a good calendar to organize the craziness that is my life, and a friend who teaches organization and goal setting had just written a blog about her 5 favorite planners. First on the list: The Passion Planner. I visited their website and found two amazing stories. One was about how the company was founded, and the other was about how, with every planner sold, one is donated to a person in need.

Sirens went off. Those angels were dancing again. I placed my order. But that's not where my experience ended. I became an ambassador for the company. I use them as an example of Cause Marketing (I'll define that later) in my speeches. I tell friends about the company and how they are the best planners on the planet. And, I'm writing about it here. Their story was simple, it was clear, and it got my emotional buy-in. They've got a loyal customer and an unpaid salesperson.

In case you were wondering which planner was number two on the list... I have no idea! I stopped reading. Were the other ones better? Who knows. Passion Planner got me.

Rule # 4: Human

In Everybody Writes, Handley says that you should "focus on how your products or services touch the lives of actual people." She's suggesting this to prevent business-to-business companies from avoiding the emotional aspects of stories and talking in generalities and corporate-speak that will bore the pants off of the audience. I just want to go one step further as the animal-loving freak that I am. Human emotions are not unique to humans. Your story (especially if you are soliciting donations for your animal rescue or if you are selling pet products) may not actually have people in it. Think back to that Budweiser commercial in Chapter Two.

Or if there are, they may not be the hero of your story. Having an animal, a plant, or even an inanimate object that you've bestowed human emotions upon ("anthropomorphized," if you want to use the fancy word), can still hook the audience and help sell your product. If you saw a commercial with a car choking on bad oil, and maybe a tear slips out of his headlight, you would likely feel bad for the car and choose a quality oil when you lube up your vehicle. Just sayin'.

Make sure your emotions are human even if your main character isn't.

Rule # 5: Serve the Customer

Remember in the Introduction, when I told you about my divorce, but promised that it was for a reason? Did I deliver on it? I hope so, because this book isn't about me. Sure, I've got some personal stories in here, but none just for the sake of telling them. The stories have a purpose. Even if you (my reader) are not involved in the story first-hand, there is a lesson to be learned and a way for you to apply it to your business. I've heard successful speakers say, "No one wants to hear your stories." That's not entirely true. Sure, no one wants to hear your stories just for poops and giggles (I'm really trying not to curse in this book so if it comes off like I'm teaching kindergarten, don't hold it against me). People want to hear your stories so they can apply the lessons to their own lives, and sometimes just to feel better about their own lives.

When you tell a story in a sales setting, the same is true. Find a story that your customer can see themselves in. Then, and only then, will the story resonate with your audience and make them want to buy whatever solution you are selling.

Rule # 6: Bigger Strategy

It's great to have quality, entertaining, simple stories, but if they are all over the place, willy-nilly, what-is-going-on-here, stories... they will lose their power.

All of your stories, from your Origin (I'll explain that term in a bit) to your ongoing narrative should support your overall business strategy. Apple is a great example of this (as they are of many things). From the very beginning, Apple positioned themselves as destroying the status quo, ushering in a new era of technology, and thinking outside the box. Nothing supports this overarching theme more than their 1984 Macintosh Commercial. If you've never seen this, hop over to YouTube for a moment and take a gander. Just don't get pulled down the rabbit hole!

Do you have goosebumps? No matter how many times I've seen that video (and it's shown in just about every marketing class ever) I get all bumpy. From the creepy dystopian future to the militant vibe, to the sledgehammer-yielding blonde lady... oooooh, she could use a flashlight on there. Apple is not like every other company. They proved it to us in 59 seconds. Did I think it was real? No. Did it tap into my emotions and make me put on a sweater? Yes.

Figure out what narrative your business wants to tell and support it with every story you craft.

And we're done! Your inner rebel can now come out from under the table. Are there exceptions to every rule? Probably. Do you need to learn the rules before you can break them? Absolutely.

CHAPTER FIVE
THAT'S NOT MY JOB

There was a meme floating around Facebook a few months back of a yellow line going down the side of the road. It was perfectly straight except for where a tree branch had fallen into the road. In that spot, the line drawer (yeah, they probably have a real name. No, I'm not going to bother to look it up) veered off course and drew his line around the fallen branch. The text at the bottom of the picture said: "Not my job."

When it comes to storytelling for business, you may be sitting back in your chair stroking your beard (or pretending you have a beard) and saying, "That's not my job."

I'm about to give you an answer that I, in a future chapter, will yell at you for using.

Who is responsible for telling stories in a company?

Everyone.

In The Strategic Storyteller (2017), Jutkowitz says, "As digital technology breaks down the barriers between jobs, sooner or later all of us will be asked to tell stories in the course of our professional lives. We will be asked to make a case for ourselves, our work, our companies, and our future."

Whether your business card reads "Salesperson", "CEO" or "Janitor," you will be called upon to sell. Maybe you won't sell products or services, but you will sell ideas. And the best way to sell those ideas is by incorporating story into your world.

Thankfully, story has always been there. Remember in Chapter One how we talked about wearing your superhero PJs (mine were She-Ra, Princess of Power) and waiting for your parents to read stories to you?

They whisked your imagination off to far away worlds where anything was possible. They entertained you and helped your creative brain develop, most importantly, they taught you values, morals, and how to behave in society. All through story. You could even say that those morals were a Call to Action.

When your company tells a story, it's not just an entertaining tale that gets shared at corporate retreats and on your About page. This story must become a central pillar of your organization. It is the North Star by which every employee will make decisions, and it is the experience that your customer will have when they walk through the door.

You might even say that it outlines and reiterates the values, morals, and how your employees behave in society. (Hmm... where have I heard that before?)

Your frontline employees, Valet Attendants, Greeters, Stock Clerks, Cashiers, and Bellboys, may not have "sales" anywhere in their job description, but they represent your organization and therefore they must be a part of the story. I know I jumped around a bunch of industries, I just want you to understand that every single employee you have — even the one locked away in the Server Room, who never sees the light of day — every employee must know, understand, and live and breathe your brand story.

Peter Guber talks about the "Westfield-as-hero" story that their shopping centers uphold in his book Tell to Win (2010). They've thought of every detail to make sure that their customers have a first-rate experience. Everything from lights over the parking spaces to see what's available and save time, to unbelievably clean break rooms for their customers with children (women with children are their largest market). In order to uphold this story, it has to be well known throughout the company.

> The first contact the customer has is usually with the least paid, lowest person on the rung who works at the location. It could be the security person. So the security person better be well trained. You've got to tell them, "Customers will tell you what they think and you've got to listen to them. You've got to be empathetic and then you've

got to be sympathetic. You do those three things and you'll find out what they want. Only when you know what they want can you exceed their expectations." In other words, you can't be your audience's hero unless you're interested in your audience.

Let's head back to you now: a salesperson (of any sort). You have one job. Your job is to evoke emotion in the buyer. Now, you may think that your responsibilities extend beyond that, and while they do in a way, everything stems from your ability to evoke emotion. First, you must show your potential customer how much they are hurting. You need to tap into their pain. Without this step, you won't get anywhere. You won't be able to show them that your product is the cure, and you certainly won't be able to ask them for the sale.

According to Godin, "All successful stories are the same. They all promise to fulfill the wishes of a consumer's worldview. They may offer a shortcut, a miracle, money, social success, safety, ego, fun, pleasure, or belonging."

Think about why you buy things. When you dive down deep into the root cause of every purchase, you'll find a pain point that is solved by one of these promises. (You can also play on fear but we'll talk about that later in the Success and Failure story.)

Yeah, my parents read to me as a kid, but I'm not a storyteller!

Sure you are. Maybe you aren't a *good* storyteller, but you are, for sure, a storyteller. From that very first bedtime story.

When I was 12 years old, we got a mini-dachshund named Woodstock. She was the cutest pup in the world (I'm getting major stink eye from my dog, Akasha as I type this — until you, Akasha. Until you.). Anyway, Woodstock used to love to sit on the couch with us and snuggle. Sometimes, she'd be sitting on the couch staring at the television when we got home, presumably wishing she could use the remote with her paws. Well, one day I decided to eat a rather large cookie from the bakery. I sat down on the couch with the cookie (in its paper bag), a napkin, and a knife. I wanted to cut it up into smaller pieces.

Now you probably already know where this is going, but my pre-pubescent brain did not comprehend that using a paper bag as a cutting board wasn't a great plan. As expected, the knife sliced through the cookie, right through the paper bag, and into the couch cushion. In a panic, I flipped the cushion and looked around the room for a furry little scapegoat.

There she was. Her big brown eyes staring up at me as if to say, "You're seriously going to pin this on me?"

I did. A few weeks later, my mom flipped the cushion (possibly because I had stained it) and discovered the slit in the fabric. With a look of pure innocence, I concocted a story about how the dog and I were playing and she jumped up onto the couch, landing at just the right angle, just long enough after her last pawdicure, to damage the fabric.

Woodstock has been gone for twelve years now, but I still live with the guilt of my betrayal.

This is the first time these words have ever been spoken or written aloud, and I'm sure that when my mom reads this, she will be filled with horror and disappointment.

Chances are, you too, made up stories as a child. If you had younger siblings, you may not have relied on the poor family dog as your fall guy (unless you didn't do your homework on time), but I'd be willing to bet you had to make up a story at some point.

I'm not asking you to lie to your customers or blame anything on the dog. I just want you to know that:

1) You are responsible for telling stories no matter what position you hold in your company

and

2) You already know how.

You are primed for story, whether you like it or not. Now it's time to embrace it and learn how to do it properly.

Part 2
How to Craft Stories

CHAPTER SIX
NO, THE ANSWER ISN'T "EVERYONE"

Before you set out to write your first word, you'll have to answer an all-important question:

"Who is your audience?" Who does your product or service help?

If you are human, your first answer was probably an overly enthusiastic, "Everyone!"

BUZZ (that's the sound of the game show buzzer).

I'm sorry. You are incorrect. Do not pass Go, do not collect $200. You are the weakest link. Goodbye.

I know, it's very tempting. You aren't even saying that to be coy or full of yourself. You truly believe that your product can change lives... all lives. That's a beautiful thing. It means you are passionate about what you do and you want to make the world a better place.

Unfortunately, you can't help everyone. But even more importantly, you can't market to everyone. When you try to speak to the world, no one will hear you. Imagine you are the hot dog guy at a baseball game. There you are, standing on the field with your backpack full o' hot dogs. You want to get the attention of everyone. You scream. You wave your arms. You jump up and down. To no avail. The roar of the crowd is impossibly loud and no one is even batting an eyelash at your screaming.

Now imagine that you are in the same stadium, same bag o' hot dogs. You scream and wave your arms, but this time it's different. First, because you are walking through the sections, directing your calls to one group at a time. Second, because there is a hungry person in a seat not too far away. He's got a problem (he was late leaving work and didn't have a chance to eat dinner) and you've got a solution (hot dogs and maybe some chips or whatever else hot dog guys carry in that backpack). Hungry guy hears your call, you send a soggy-bun-covered dog his way, and you both continue on your merry way having made a connection that is positive for both of you.

Storytelling for sales is a bit like that interaction. You need to know who you are looking to talk to (your ideal client), and they have to be willing to listen (because they have a need). Head back to the stands for one more minute. Here you are, hot dog man, screaming to the hungry guy. You may be talking directly to him, but the people around him can hear you too. In fact, one of them didn't realize it at first, but he's hungry too. Now that he sees the dog heading towards his neighbor, he decides he'd like a snack as well.

When you "speak" to a specific person, to an ideal client, other people still hear you. They aren't going to say "Well you know, he wasn't really talking to me so I probably can't go buy his (insert whatever you sell here). If your product or service is useful for them, they will buy it.

Convinced you have to speak to someone in particular? Good. If you aren't convinced yet, go back and read my subpar sports metaphor a few more times. Now that this is established, how do you go about defining your audience?

While I've never chosen to fight crime for a living, I wanted to be an FBI Profiler when I was younger. I went to school for Forensic Psychology and prepared myself to enter the mind of a killer. (No, Criminal Minds wasn't out yet, but I sure was obsessed with it once it started). Anyway, I only got to use my actual profiling skills once, though the case wasn't very hard to crack.

I had recently moved to Las Vegas and was still living with my parents. It was almost Christmastime and for months I'd been collecting stuffed animals to donate to Toys for Tots. Whenever I saw something cute on sale, I added it to the pile. One day, I returned home from an awful day substitute teaching. When I say awful, I mean an "I had a student light his pants on fire" kind of day. It was bad. All I wanted to do was go home, snuggle up with my furry, little princess

Akasha, and de-stress from the horrendous assignment.

That was not in the cards.

My father met me at the door with a concerned look on his face. He didn't say anything, he just led me to my room and stood outside the door as I examined the carnage. Every surface from the floor to the furniture was covered in white fluff. There were lifeless eyes staring up in horror and plastic noses strewn about. It would later be known as the Great Stuffed Animal Massacre of 2009.

My training kicked in.

I examined the crime scene. There were signs of a brutal attack. The victims were taken by surprise, no time to fight back. Who could do something like this? The UNSUB had to be stealthy in order to sneak up on the stuffed animals. He or she had to have some latent anger. Perhaps they hadn't been walked recently. Maybe they just didn't get a Scooby Snack that day. I searched high and low for an individual who fit the profile... and there she was.

My dog Akasha had returned to the scene of the crime, a small bit of white fluff lodged in the corner of her snout. Thanks to my education, I was able to solve the case.

What does this have to do with your audience? Well, in Forensics (both the psychology and science) you have to work backward. You look at the end result and see what kind of person (or Beagle/Lab mix) would commit a certain act. In sales, that "certain act" is buying your product. What kind of person would buy your product? How old are they? What do they do for a living? Do they have a family? You need to step into your customer's shoes and get into their head.

I've heard this described as an ideal customer, a buyer persona, an Alex, and about a million other names. Whatever you call it, you need to have a picture of your perfect customer in your head, and whenever you open your mouth (or put pen to page or fingers to keyboard), you need to speak to them. It will change the tone of your story and the words you use. Don't believe me? Go volunteer at the library to read to children and bring along a copy of Fifty Shades of Gray.

Wrong. Audience.

(OMG don't do that! I'm just making a point here. Please do not get arrested because of this book).

"Everyone" does not need your product. And even if they do, no one responds to "Hey Everyone!". I have a friend who sells skincare. When she was instructing our networking group on who her ideal customer would be, she said "Anyone with skin." Cute, but not entirely true. The people that buy this brand of skincare are within a specific income bracket. Any less and they wouldn't be able to afford it. Any more and they would probably be purchasing designer skincare that comes with the prestige of spending too much because you can.

The most important part of classifying your ideal client is

finding someone who is looking for a solution to a problem that you can help them with. Maybe you are developing a buyer persona for your new light-up ax: Mr. Woodsy. You've decided that Mr. Woodsy is male and between the ages of 30 and 45. He lives alone and makes hats for squirrels for a living, which he then sells at the flea market five towns over. He nets about 10k per year (there isn't much demand for squirrel hats). You've done your homework and you know exactly who you are speaking to. Mr. Woodsy would be the perfect customer to purchase your light-up ax. There's just one problem...

Mr. Woodsy's mom used to read <u>The Lorax</u> to him every night and he doesn't believe in cutting down trees. He uses old newspapers to heat his cabin. Your ideal customer isn't actually looking for your product. Or perhaps, he just likes to use his old ax plus a headlamp to cut down his trees (sorry, Lorax). It's working for him so why would he do anything different?

Godin talks about worldviews in <u>All Marketers are Liars</u> (2012). Worldviews are "rules, values, beliefs, and biases that an individual consumer brings to a situation." Now the worldview that Mr. Woodsy falls into, and one you might face when identifying your audience, is called "If it ain't broke, don't fix it."

> The reason so many effective solutions take forever to get implemented is that the fear of change is greater than the cost of sticking with what you've got. In other words, people wait until they have a heart attack or get

diabetes before they go on a diet.

You can't change a worldview. Before you put hours, days, or weeks of work into crafting your story, identify your ideal customer and the audience you will be speaking to. This will help you nail the correct tone for your stories and have potential clients remarking, "It was like they were talking directly to me. Like they already knew me."

Now it's not a story, but I just got an email from Chewy.com. I ordered some food for my dog and just received one of the best emails of my life. They gave me the information I needed about my order and then closed out the email with:

Give us a bark if there's anything else we can help your furry pal with. Sending paw-sitive vibes Akasha's way.

Tail wags & kibble bags,

Ummm... wow. If they didn't nail the tone for their ideal customer (pet parent who adores their fur baby and may or may not sing lullabies to them at three in the morning when they've had a nightmare - don't judge me), I don't know what possibly could.

The coupon was nice, the food I can get almost anywhere, but they just wowed the heck out of me with three sentences. Wouldn't it be nice to know your audience that well?

CHAPTER SEVEN
WHATCHA GONNA TALK ABOUT, WILLIS?

It's super important to tell stories, but not just any stories. Please don't ever sit down with potential clients and start a story with "This one time... at band camp..."

Every story you tell should have a purpose. Not just a Call to Action, but a deliberate, "I'm going to tell this story because" reason behind it. Let's take a quick look at the 3ish (I'll explain that, I promise) types of stories that you need to have in your arsenal, and what they do to establish you as a force to be reckoned with. They are:

1) Origin Story

2) Success (or Failure)

3) Cause Marketing

Origin Story

The term "origin story" actually finds its roots in the comic book industry. It describes the deep dive into a specific character's background that gives the audience insight into what makes them tick. In the early versions of my keynote, I used X-Men and Wolverine as an example. Turns out the best part of that example is me floundering to explain what the X-Men are to a room full of people that have never watched the movie or (egad) read the comic book.

Though Wolverine with his metal claws is an amazing example of this, I'll spare you the explanation (mostly because I can't make awkward hand movements and faces in a book) and we'll examine a story that you are sure to have seen at some point.

Superman. You've seen that, right? Read the comic book? Seen the nine million movies and T.V. shows that were made from it? Anyone? Bueller? If you haven't... I can't help you! Go watch Superman and then come back and keep reading.

Let's dive in. When you start watching Superman, you are introduced to this super-strong dude whose greatest power (in my opinion) is his ability to disguise his real identity with a pair of glasses and some pomade. You may be thinking to yourself, "Why is he so incredibly strong?" or "Why does he appear to be afraid of rocks?" or maybe even "Where is this guy when I need to open a jar of tomato sauce?"

Then we get to his origin story. Superman (aka Clark Kent

when he doesn't glue down his hair) was born as Kal-El on an alien planet called Krypton. Knowing that their planet was about to be destroyed, his parents fashioned a spacecraft, packed their baby up and sent him drifting into the ether. Shards of the planet survive as kryptonite and become the one thing that can actually hurt him.

Why did I just tell you this?

Well, you didn't have much of an emotional connection to Superman in the beginning. In fact, if you are a bodybuilder, you were probably pretty jealous of his 0% body fat. But as soon as you learned about his history, it triggered the "Awww Factor." His parents died saving him? Awww. The only thing that can kill him are remnants of his old life (deeper meaning alert). Awww. You, my friend, have just developed an emotional connection with a superhero. You understand where he came from and why he does what he does (to protect his new home planet since he lost his old one), and you have a vested interest in his future.

The purpose of the Origin Story is to share your Why with your audience. There is a great TED talk out there by Simon Sinek where he discusses the importance of your Why. If you'd like to check it out, it's called How Great Leaders Inspire Action. It's about 18 minutes long and well worth the time. Go ahead. I've got some laundry that needs to be folded. Meet you back here in a few.

Welcome back!

Did you love it? If you didn't watch it (or even if you did), my biggest take away from the talk is that "People don't buy what you do, they buy why you do it."

Boom.

Why did you open your business? Why does (insert your industry here) appeal to you? Let's look at a few examples from the real world.

1) The animal rescue I volunteer with was opened because of the founder's daughter. Christy (the founder) read a journal entry that her daughter Kendall wrote in school. The prompt was: If I had one wish... Ten-year-old Kendall said that if she had one wish, it would be to open an animal rescue called Hearts Alive Village and save everything from dogs and cats to cows and horses. When Christy read the journal entry, she asked Kendall if this was really her wish.

"Yes, it is, but I know it would be too hard," said Kendall.

Christy's heart nearly split open. She didn't want her daughter growing up believing that dreams are too hard. We are a few farm animals short of Kendall's dream, but give us some time.

2) The founder of Canine Assistants, Jennifer Arnold, was diagnosed with multiple sclerosis as a teenager. She spent two years in a wheelchair asking for help and apologizing for her condition. When her father found out about an organization on the West Coast that trained service dogs to help people in wheelchairs, they decided to open their own on the East Coast. Two weeks later, her father was killed by

a drunk driver. It took ten years but she and her mother finally opened the organization and have now provided over 1500 service dogs (free of charge) to people with disabilities.

3) A friend of mine is a distributor for a diet program. A few years ago, he was 60 pounds overweight. He had no energy for his business, his doctor was threatening cholesterol medication, and his kids kept asking, "Daddy, why don't you want to play with us?"

Then he found this diet program. He lost the weight and got his life and his family back and now he helps other people do the same. I don't have the slightest idea "how" his program works. But whenever I think of weight loss, whenever I come across someone talking about their need to diet, I think of him.

Now the reason that I said there were "3ish" stories, is that if you aren't the founder of your company, you'll need your own Why Story. The best example I can give for this is one of my coaching clients. He works for an organization that provides training and employment services to ex-cons. When I asked him to tell me about what he does, he regurgitated the About page from the website.

"That tells me why the organization was founded, but it doesn't tell me why you work there," I said.

It took some poking, prodding, and a lot of emotional support, but he finally told me why he worked there. Turns out that he had been arrested years earlier. He'd lost his job, his family, and his life as he knew it. This organization had been the reason that he was matriculated back into society instead of reoffending.

Now, if you were sitting across from this man contemplating whether or not you wanted to donate to his organization, would you be swayed by the story from the website, or by the fact that he was passionate about what he does because it saved his life? Telling your story takes quite a bit of vulnerability, but it pays off. We'll get to that a little bit later.

The power of your business, the piece that sets you apart from your competitors, is your why.

Success (or Failure) Story

Ideally, you'll have more than one of these, but it's okay to dip your toe into storytelling and start out with one signature Success story.

Does your product or service work? Does it do what it claims to do? If my weight loss friend was still 60 pounds overweight, I'd be less likely to buy from him. A Success story is a narrative about a customer that had a problem, found your solution, and now they are living happily ever after. Yep, it's seriously that simple. A realtor hired me to write the content for his website. It was super flashy, graphically decked out, and no one stayed on it for more than 2 minutes. That's because there was no substance. I wrote some catchy content, added some informational blogs, explained his Origin Story, and now people stick around for longer and actually call to hire him. Success.

Remember sweet little Gemma from the beginning of this book? In my opinion, she is one of the greatest success stories of our animal rescue. Whisked from the brink of death, she now lives the life of luxury.

You might be wondering, "If Success stories are so simple, why would you tell a failure story?"

Think of it more as a cautionary tale. It's the "What happens when you don't hire me" story that convinces people they need what you are selling. Unfortunately, I've got an amazing one.

My friend Joe used to sell Life Insurance. Insurance, in general, is one of those things that you never want to think about, and you hope you never need, but when you do... boy, do you need it.

His friend (we'll call him John just so you have a detail to anchor with) came into his office one day to discuss purchasing a policy. John was a construction worker with a wife and two children.

"I drive back and forth to California every week for work. If anything ever happens to me, I just want to make sure that my family is taken care of."

Joe recommended a one million dollar policy that would cover his funeral costs, pay off the mortgage on the house, care for the family, and if treated properly, would help the children with college expenses. John was on board and the paperwork was drawn up. It was sitting on Joe's desk waiting for John to come in and sign, and pay the first month's premium. And there it stayed. Joe called him every few weeks for eight months, but John kept hemming and hawing as to whether the policy was worth paying for each month.

One day, John was returning from a construction job in California when the tire blew on his truck. His truck flipped and he was killed instantly.

Instead of his wife having the money to keep the family comfortable, Joe had to start a crowdfunding campaign so they could bury John and keep the house out of foreclosure.

It's okay to warn your audience of the dangers of *not* doing business with you.

And now on to my favorite type of story...

Cause Marketing

Let's switch gears now. Take your business owner-hat off for a moment and put on your consumer hat. Raise your hand if you have ever or would ever stop doing business with a company because they supported something you were really against? I don't want to get political so can we safely say that everyone reading this cares somewhat about the environment? Okay, so what if a company was dumping toxic sewage into our water supply? You'd probably stop giving them your money, right?

So let's turn that around. Would you be more likely to use a service or buy a product from a company that supported things you do care about? Welcome to Cause Marketing.

If you exist in the corporate arena, you've probably heard the term "Corporate Social Responsibility." That will be the last time you hear that term in my book. I'm just not a fan. I prefer to describe Cause Marketing as the sale of warm fuzzies.

Let me explain. Let's say that you sell widgets. You started selling widgets because you saw a need for widgets in the market and you decided to meet that need. (By the way, that's not a very exciting Origin story. Now if a widget saved your mother from certain death, you've got a good Origin story). Your widgets work and you've had many happy customers for whom widgets have made a true difference in their lives. You've got some good Success stories. But let's be honest, widgets are not exciting. Widgets are not sexy. Widgets are just... seriously, what are widgets? I feel like they were something in the Jetsons. Anyway, there's nothing fun about selling widgets.

Thankfully, the owner of Widgetmart (we'll call her Susan) is also very philanthropic. She fully believes in serving her community and finds the rates of food insecurity in her town, especially among children, to be unacceptable. Maybe she grew up poor and remembers those days of being called to the Main Office to collect the canned goods her classmates had donated.

Susan is about to discover the power of Cause Marketing. She pledges 1% of her gross sales to support her local food bank. She spends her Saturday mornings at soup kitchens serving the homeless. She has donation boxes set up in her employee break rooms and gives comp time to her employees who want to volunteer. She has also switched her commercials from a description of the widget-making process to a story about how her employees give back to the community and how they've served over 6,000 meals in the last year. Susan is no longer selling widgets... now she's selling warm fuzzies.

Let's look at the many benefits of Cause Marketing, which if done correctly, will change the future of your business.

1) You do a good thing for the community. Whatever your religion, faith, spirituality may be, this is a plus. Yay for karma!

2) You develop a reputation in the community as being about more than just money. Customers gravitate towards companies that support their values and want to do business with people who are making a difference in the community. The 2017 Cone Cause Evolution Study found that:

- 70% of consumers believe companies have an obligation to take actions to improve issues that may not be relevant to everyday business operations.
- 92% have a more positive image of a product or company when it supports a cause they care about.

Shortly after the 2016 presidential election, I got my Yoga magazine out of the mailbox and as always, flipped to the back cover (am I the only one that reads magazines from back to front?). There was a full-page ad from Jade Yoga explaining that due to the changing social climate, they would be putting more of their money behind causes that needed extra support like the EPA, Planned Parenthood, and the NAACP. You can bet that they earned a lot of customers off of that ad, and it had nothing to do with yoga accessories.

3) You will increase your visibility, getting yourself in front of audiences that normally wouldn't see you. The charity has a vested interest in promoting your business and driving customers to you. The charity will do everything in their power to advertise your product. People that have never heard of you, are now made aware of not just your product or your service, but your willingness to support a cause they love.

Let's talk about ice cream for a minute. My friend Leif owns Momenti Spirited Ice Creams, a company that makes alcoholic ice cream and sorbets. I'll give you a moment to process that. Aside from making the most amazing ice cream ever, his business model includes partnering with non-profits that align with his values. Two years ago in December, they partnered with Send me on Vacation, a charity supporting survivors of breast cancer, and New Vista, who helps the developmentally disabled. They created two new flavors, Bourbon Eggnog and Rum Raisin, and gave a portion of the sales to the charities. Remember that this is December — not the high season for ice cream. They made over $7,000 in one month, doubling their usual sales — even in a good month. They spent $0 on advertising. In March, the animal rescue I'm with had a big charity show called Mondays Dark. Leif created a special flavor for us called Bark Bark Batter and came to the show and served it in exchange for donations to the rescue. When Leif created the flavor, I went over to his factory and videotaped my taste test. I then posted the video on my rescue's Facebook page and it got over 1,000 hits. One thousand people who many never have tried his ice cream, learned about his product and his commitment to helping the community because of one batch of ice cream.

4) You get to "borrow" a non-profit's story, which beefs up your own story.

5) You can charge more for your product.

Now I don't want to throw any companies under the bus (actually, I'd love to, but I don't want to get sued). A few months ago, I was perusing my Yoga magazine and saw a cute t-shirt. I popped over to the company's website to see if it was in my budget. It was $79. Seventy-freakin'-nine dollars. I frantically surfed the site looking for a charitable connection. Surely $40 of my purchase was going to build wells in Africa so people could have fresh water. Maybe it would provide school supplies for children in need. Or every time you bought a t-shirt, they donated a truckload of chew toys to shelter dogs. I clicked from page to page... it had to be there somewhere.

But it wasn't.

My $79 would go into their bank account, and there it would stay. I'll spare you the stream of superlatives that came out of my mouth (I did promise not to curse in this book), and leave it at: Oh Heck No!

Now, if that t-shirt company was pocketing $25 or even $35 and then giving the rest to a non-profit, I would've been entering my credit card number. I'm not alone. The Nielsen Global Survey of Corporate Social Responsibility and Sustainability conducted in 2015 showed that 66% of consumers are willing to pay extra for products and services that come from companies that are committed to positive social and environmental impact. The Millennials CSR Study by Cone Communications found that 70% of Millennials (ages 18-34) would be willing to pay more. The Nielson Global Survey of Corporate Social Responsibility and Sustainability.

6) You'll beat out your competitors.

Remember that awesome planner I told you about? When I discovered that they had a Buy One-Give One program and that when I purchased my planner, one would be donated to someone less fortunate, I was sold. The other planners may have been better, I honestly never even looked. This company allowed me to help others so it was a no-brainer for me.

"When price and quality are equal, we know most consumers (89% according to the study) will choose the product benefiting the cause," explains Alison DaSilva, executive vice president at Cone.

Still not convinced? Here's the conclusion of the Cone Study:

> Today's complex political environment combined with the pressing challenges facing the globe, leave Americans wondering where to turn next. The 2017 Cone Communications CSR study reveals Americans are giving companies not only the invitation but the mandate to step up to solve today's most complex social and environmental issues.
>
> In order to lead as a responsible company, it's simply not enough to address internal operation challenges — businesses must take the lead to push progress on issues that go straight to the hearts and minds of Americans and communicate company values in a way that's relevant and authentic. Today's consumers are smart and empowered. They have a propensity to dig in to do their own research. They are willing to use their voice and dollars as a force for change, becoming a company's staunchest supporters — or detractors. Now is the time to not only stand for but stand up for something that matters.

Like every rule, there are exceptions. And sometimes these exceptions blow up in your face.

Remember Godin's concept of a "worldview?" In case you

forgot, they are the "rules, values, beliefs, and biases that an individual consumer brings to a situation." Let's use a fictional character to understand this better. Did you ever watch <u>A Christmas Carol</u>? I'm going to refer to the Muppet version because that's how I roll. It's okay if you've never seen it. I'm pretty sure they stuck pretty close to Charles Dickens' classic story.

Here you've got Ebenezer Scrooge. He's a cranky ol' bastard who refuses to give his frog and rat employees enough coal so they don't freeze their tails off during the winter. (Do frogs have tails? Freeze his flippers off?)

Anyway, he gets a visit from Beaker and Bunsen who are collecting donations for the poor. The conversation goes like this:

Bunsen: Hey, now then sir, about the donation?
Scrooge: Well now, let's see. I know how to treat the poor. My taxes go to pay for the prisons and the poorhouses. The homeless must go there.
Bunsen: But some would rather die.
Scrooge: If they would rather die, they had better do it, and decrease the surplus population.

Scrooge doesn't have a very philanthropic attitude, and if you were going to use a Cause Marketing story, he would not be your audience. Unless of course, you have 3 ghosts on retainer... in which case you may be able to change his worldview.

Now just because your ideal customer doesn't believe in

giving back to the community, doesn't mean you shouldn't do it. I am a firm believer that every business should be connected to a cause. In fact, a portion of the proceeds from this book and a percentage of every speaking engagement I do is donated to Hearts Alive Village Animal Rescue. Look at that, you are learning how to tell stories and you helped some fuzz butts in the process.

Earlier, I mentioned Jade Yoga and their support of certain non-profits after the presidential election. They drew a very firm line in the sand with their support and I have no doubt that they earned loyal customers because of it. However, I'm pretty sure they also lost some. If a segment of their customers were Pro-Life, you can bet that they packed up their sweat rags and headed for another yoga mat company.

The Cone Study found that 76% of consumers would refuse to purchase a product if they found out a company supported an issue contrary to their beliefs. Right now, just weeks after another school shooting, the fight around gun control is raging on. In the past few days, I have seen the same declaration, refusing to sell firearms, from Dick's Sporting Goods posted along with comments ranging from "I'll never shop at Dicks again," to "I'm glad companies are stepping up to protect our children."

I've stopped patronizing businesses on many occasions because of their beliefs and behavior. Trophy hunting, refusing to provide birth control for employees, discriminating against the LGBT community, destroying our environment... I refuse to support companies that I don't morally agree with.

As a business owner (or just a human being), you'll never make everyone happy. You aren't a jar of Nutella. (I wish I could take credit for that but I found it on the interweb, source unknown). Stand for whatever it is that you care about, tell a good story, and you'll attract your tribe.

CHAPTER EIGHT
THERE'S GOLD IN THEM THAR HILLS!

"Great stories happen to those who can tell them." - Ira Glass

Maybe you've made it this far through the book and are thinking, "This is cool, and I would do it... but nothing interesting ever happens to me."

Hogwash!

I've always wanted to say that—that felt good. The world is full of stories. Your life is full of stories. If you look hard enough, every story has a moral. Allow me to explain.

I remember the day that I learned this lesson. I had just started blogging for myself. Mind you, I'd been blogging for other companies for years at this point, but this was the first time that I was using my own experiences to teach a lesson. As I'm prone to doing when I get stressed, I ransacked my pantry looking for a piece of chocolate. I couldn't wait to have the heavenly goodness melt in my mouth and to stop the nervous twitch that develops when it's been too long since my last feeding. It was just a few weeks after my birthday and a friend had gotten me a chocolate assortment to wish me a happy day. I'd squirreled it away for an emergency situation just like today. It was the Russian Roulette-style variety pack where you had no idea what you were getting until it was too late.

I bit into the chocolate and was assaulted by a coconut crème filling (I like neither coconut nor creme). I proceeded to spit the chocolate out, and then dramatically swish water around my mouth while my dog watched me and snickered. Gross.

I could've given up and headed back up to my office, unsatisfied and angry from my chocolate fail. But I didn't. I grabbed another piece of chocolate and tried again! And this time, it was caramel and all was right with the world. In life, when you try and fail, don't give up. Just try again. Or, you know, as the great Forrest Gump sais, "Life is like a box of chocolates. You never know what you're going to get."

From then on, I realized that blogging didn't have to be so difficult. You don't need dramatic or traumatic experiences to learn a lesson or even to change the course of your life.

Bam! Life lesson served up with cocoa butter and sugar. I took an everyday activity (sometimes multiple times per day depending on my stress level) and turned it into a story with a life lesson. We'll examine the elements of a story in the next chapter so, for now, you'll just have to trust me that it had everything you need.

So where will you find your stories? Let's focus on Success stories first.

One of the biggest concerns I hear (and have voiced myself) is, "I'm new in this field and I don't have any of my own stories of helping customers or clients."

That's fair. Here I am telling you that you need to tell Success stories and you may not have any. We've all been there. Everyone was brand new at some point, even the greats. Do you think Tony Robbins woke up one morning having helped millions of people? Nope. One day, he made a conscious decision to start charging for what he was probably already doing for friends and family. There are a few ways you can handle your wet-behind-the-ears situation.

1) Use a story of someone you helped for free. I've told a few stories in this book so far and none of them have started out with "My client who paid X amount of dollars for my service..." No one needs to know if you charged for the service you provided. If you are a coach, maybe you used your skills and method on your college roommate and that's the moment you realized you had a gift. If you are an accountant, maybe you did your own taxes after the CPA had done them and found a way to save yourself some money. You are now the "client". You aren't lying. You

actually helped someone and achieved results. Peter Guber talks about the different ways you can relate to a story in Tell To Win (2010) and this falls under the "Firsthand experience". You lived it and you are telling the audience what you experienced.

2) Borrow a story from a coworker... and give them credit! If you have joined a company and are selling on behalf of a larger brand, your coworkers, mentors, and friends are a treasure trove of material. Ask them to describe some of the experiences they've had, the customer issues they've resolved, what they consider to be their biggest wins. Just make sure that when you relate this story to your potential clients, you begin with, "One of my coworkers once..." You always want to be on the up and up and you never want to use a standard, hackneyed industry story as your own. There is nothing worse than having a potential customer say, "That's interesting, I was just at another (insert your industry here) and they told me the same story." Groan. Headbanging shame. Remember how hoodwinked I felt when I read the car rental story by two different people? Don't let this be you.

If you are lucky enough to watch these stories unfold, you can put your own spin on them and bring the audience along on a journey through your eyes. Later this year, I will be featured in a documentary about my divorce experience. The founder of the Unstuck brand, John Polish, will be narrating the film and asked the videographer if it was okay for him to narrate even though he wasn't there when I (and a few others) had their experience. The videographer suggested that he tell our stories through his eyes. What did he think when he first met us? How did he feel learning about the tragedies we had undergone. Guber would likely file this under the "Witnessed experience". You saw it (or are being told secondhand) and you are telling the audience what you saw and felt.

3) Find stories that don't necessarily relate to the product, but support the theme or the Call to Action that you'd like to put forth. One of the World Champions of Public Speaking, Ed Tate, tells a story about being a "Break-it-Yourself-er." Apparently, one day he decided that he had the skills necessary to fix his in-ground sprinkler system. A ravaged yard, an embarrassing phone call, and several thousand dollars later, his sprinkler was fixed. (Though his marriage never recovered). Ed isn't selling yard maintenance or plumbing services. He's selling the idea that the journey is harder and more expensive when you go it alone. It's a perfect segue into his offer for coaching. According to Guber, this is the "Metaphor/ Analogy."

Now that the newbies no longer feel lost and sad, let's talk about the richest source of your success stories... customer testimonials.

I had struggled with finding my message and my "expertise" for several years at the beginning of my speaking career. I watched all of my emerging speaker friends enjoy their ah-ha moment and head off into the wonderful world of professional speaking. They had a purpose. They had experience and knowledge in a certain field and they ran with it. I, on the other hand, felt like a jack of all trades and a master of none. I've held every job from Customer Service Representative to Mental Health Counselor and none of them lit my fire enough to speak about it for the next forty years.

A friend of mine invited me to a writing retreat with Julie Cameron (if you need permission to be creative, grab one of her books. They are fabulous.). The weekend was in Sedona, Arizona and besides being in workshops for large chunks of each day, there was plenty of time for introspection, barefoot yoga on the magical red rocks, and this thing I've heard about... med-i-ta-tion.

I participated in a starlight meditation, heading out on the walking path with a guide who had us do a few Tai-chi exercises and then left us to our own self-discovery. It was sitting beside a lake, under the stars, that I had my epiphany. I've been a writer and a storyteller for most of my life. Surely I could help others harness the power of story to improve something tangible like their sales.

Mind. Blown. Apparently amazing things happen when I just shut up for a few minutes. Who knew?

The name Once Upon a Bottom Line popped into my head (thank you divine intervention) and something clicked. I knew this was what I was meant to do. But as I always do, I second-guessed myself. I've had other flashes of brilliant ideas (mostly when I've had too much caffeine and I'm lying awake at 3 am cursing a barista). I decided that I needed confirmation. I asked for a sign. I wanted something that would let me know, with no room for doubt, that I was on the right path.

As the guide led us back to the main retreat house, I popped in for a quick potty stop. As I was coming out of the bathroom, something caught my eye. Right next to the tea bags was a card that read:

Share your Story to Help Others

Sedona Mago Retreat values your retreat experience. Your testimonial is a wonderful tool for others to make an informed decision.
Please take a moment and tell your story at
www.sedonamagoretreat.org/testimonials

Message received. That card is now pinned to my bulletin board, a constant reminder that I'm on the right path. And now, it's reminding me that I should probably hop on their website and write a testimonial about my experience.

Your customers are an invaluable source of material for your Success stories. There is nothing more powerful than allowing satisfied customers to tell the story of the challenges they faced, and how your product or service helped to overcome them, in their own words. Give them a space to do this on your website, in your store, on review sites, and if possible, offer them an incentive. I won a 42-

inch tv a few months ago for leaving a testimonial for my dentist on Yelp.

Lead with a Story talks about an innkeeper who went above and beyond the call of duty, fishing through an industrial-sized garbage dumpster to find a lost mouth guard. The customer was so delighted that she wrote a story about it and posted it on TripAdvisor.com. When Lead with a Story was written, almost 1,000 people planning vacations had read it.

People love to talk. They love to see their name in print. And they will become your best storytellers if you give them the tools and the platform. Don't believe that your customers can influence strangers? Search Engine Land (this is an actual site, not me being sarcastic) found that approximately 72 percent of surveyed consumers indicated that they trust reviews as much as personal recommendations. 52 percent said that positive online reviews will increase the likelihood that they'll patronize a local business. 5 Non Icky Ways to Ask for Testimonials

Testimonials are incredibly powerful and while you can use these success stories in your face-to-face conversations, there are other places that they can help influence potential buyers. You can post (short) testimonial stories throughout your website or on a dedicated page. Companies like Airbnb allow hosts and visitors to share stories on their website about their experiences. They are, in effect crowdsourcing their success stories and then using them to their full advantage. Customers feel like they are a part of the company.

You can also use testimonials on LinkedIn, in your sales emails, post video testimonials on YouTube, and much more. It's okay to get creative.

In the next chapter, we'll talk about the elements you need for your stories. This will help you guide your happy customers to create a usable and powerful narrative for your service.

The Origin story is about you, so it should be fairly easy to uncover your story. If for some reason, you don't know why you do what you do, ask close family or friends who have known you for a long time and ask them if they see any correlations between your past and your current business or employment.

When it comes to aligning yourself with a non-profit and creating your Cause Marketing story, you get to tell the organization's story. But people still want to know why you care about the cause. My animal rescue has partnered with an insurance agent whose company offers a Quotes for Donations program. I met him a few years ago at a networking event and he approached me with zest and zeal, wanting to partner and help us make some money.

I've heard that before. At least three times a week, a company approaches us offering "fundraising magic." Often, they don't follow through. More often, they want us to advertise to our tribe for them, and they give us .0000001% of the purchase price. Thank you no, thank you.

But as he promised, this man called me a few days later. He'd done some research on my rescue and after years of looking for a cause that was close to his heart, he finally found us. Then, he told me his story. He'd found a pit bull running in the streets when he was a child and this dog had been his best friend, staying by his side through a difficult and painful childhood. His best friend was long gone, but the memory of comfort and love stayed with him. Now, he wanted to help this misunderstood breed in any way that he could.

And he has. He's been with us at every single event, singing our praises, sending adopters and donors our way, and raising thousands of dollars for our organization. He loves to crack jokes about how common insurance agents are "You can step onto the corner, throw a rock, and you are bound to hit an insurance agent," but he's very serious when he says that aligning with our non-profit has made his business.

Never forget to share your Why with your audience. Whether it's in your Origin Story or your Cause Marketing story, people want to connect with you as a human being before they connect with you as a business person.

And please dig deep. I worked with a website content client who ran a yoga studio and juicing business. As I always do with my clients, I mined for information. When did she first know she wanted to run these businesses? Why was she interested in health and well-being? We danced around for weeks. She kept giving me these half-assed answers like, "I don't know. I've always been interested in health." Aargh! She was a tough shell to crack but, eventually, we got to the ooey gooey insides. She had lost her father to heart disease when she was a teenager. She'd become interested in health and fitness to help her mother stay healthy and ensure that she was never in danger because of her diet. Now that is a Why.

In <u>Everybody Writes</u>, Handley suggests asking yourself the following questions when crafting your own story:

> 1) What is unique about our business?
>
> 2) What is interesting about how our business was founded? About the founder?
>
> 3) What problem is our company trying to solve?
>
> 4) What inspired our business?
>
> 5) What aha! moments has our company had?
>
> 6) How has our business evolved?
>
> 7) How do we feel about our business, our customers, ourselves?
>
> 8) What's an unobvious way to tell our story?
>
> 9) What do we consider normal and boring that other folks would think is cool?
>
> 10) And most important: relay your vision. How will our company change the world?

Need more help getting the creative juices flowing? Check

out 72 Questions to Help You Dig Deep in Telling Your Brand Story.

Crafting your story is fairly simple (but maybe not easy) if you own your own business or are trying to tell the story of why you went to work for a specific company, but what if you work for an existing company that has never taken the time to craft their own Origin Story? Jutkowitz says to look within the organization. "Don't be afraid to cast (literally cast, as a fisherman does with his line and hook) deep and wide in your organization. Look for what business writer Michael D. Watkins calls 'natural company historians.' This can be anybody from a long-time trusted administrative assistant to your chief marketing officer." Strategic Storyteller.

It may never have been written down, but someone inside of your company knows the story of why it came to be. Find that person and get every ounce of information you can get. Inspiration is all around us. Keep a story file and whenever a story comes to mind, jot down a few words to help jog your memory. You can use a notebook, a word document, or the Notes program in your phone. I use Evernote because I can jot things down in my phone and have them show up on my computer. Hooray for technology!

Give yourself permission and space to dive into your past and be honest and vulnerable with the stories you tell. You will be rewarded.

CHAPTER NINE
THREE BEARS AND ONE INDECISIVE CRIMINAL

Depending on who you ask, you'll likely get a different answer regarding the necessary elements of a story. A professional novelist, screenwriter, or playwright may give you a complex, intricate description with ups and downs, peaks and valleys, beats, or whatever else they use to describe the different elements. If you ask a child what you need to write a story, they'll likely tell you that you need a beginning, a middle, and an end.

I've got great news for you! You don't have to be in the former group to craft a business story. Yes, yes, you can whoop and holler and relax now. You needn't devise new worlds, in-depth characters, or obscenely long narratives to persuade your potential customers. In fact, doing that might actually work against you. Instead, channel your inner child. Hey! Don't leave. It's not time for finger-painting.

If you read and remember the introduction, I told you about that writing teacher after my divorce... Well, he didn't just inspire me to take action, he also gave me the best crash course in storytelling that anyone could ask for. He said that everything you needed to know about story, you could learn from Goldilocks and the Three Bears.

Hmm.

You need 5 elements for every story. We are going to dive deeper into structure in the next chapter, but for now, just know that every story needs:

1) A hero or main character (MC) - we'll get to that shortly
2) A goal
3) A conflict or something standing in the way of that goal
4) A solution
5) Emotion

Let's apply Goldilocks to our formula (ignoring the fact that she was breaking and entering):

Hero or MC: Goldilocks

Goal: She'd like to enjoy a hearty meal and get a good night's sleep

Conflict: Nothing is right. The chairs are too big or too small, the porridge is too hot or too cold, and the beds are too hard or too soft.

Solution: She finds the "just right" versions of everything she needs.

Emotion: The daddy bear growled, the baby bear cried,

Goldilocks was afraid, I think we've got emotion.

Me thinks my teacher might've been right on the money.

Before we get any further into this, I want to explain the terms "Hero" and "Main Character" , as I'll be using them interchangeably throughout this book. Normally, when you hear the term "hero," it's referring to someone who does something amazing. Maybe they are a superhero, maybe they are an ordinary person who jumped into traffic to push a stranger out of the way of a speeding car, or perhaps, they do animal rescue (shameless plug for my rescue friends). The hero of our stories will be the main character. This is the person, or animal, that the audience can follow along with on their journey. In order for them to be an effective main character, they need to be relatable and the reader must be able to identify with them and feel how they feel.

Just to give you an example, there was a commercial a few years back for McDonald's that told the story of a busy, working mom who was feeling guilty for not spending more time with her children. Can you relate to that? I don't have any human children, but there is nothing that rips my heart out faster than the sadness in my dog's eyes when I kiss her on the head and walk out the door for the day.

Thankfully, the mom has found McDonald's as a solution to her pain (not just the pain of needing to feed her children, but the pain of her guilt from having to work). She feeds her kids McNuggets and all is right with her world. She is both the hero and the main character.

Hero

Who will be the hero of your story?

Peter Guber talks about selecting a hero in <u>Tell To Win</u>. He offers 6 options for casting the main character of your story. Teller, Listener, Customer, Product, Location, Tribe. We are going to take a closer look at 4 of these:

Teller as Hero: This is generally frowned upon, especially in the speaking world, where they espouse the mantra "Never be the hero of your own story." Only cast yourself as the hero if you, "Never lose sight of what's in it for the audience, and you know you can deliver."

Listener as Hero: The story surrounding Gemma's story in the Introduction (about the potential donor), cast the potential donor as the hero. "It was because of generous contributions from community members just like him, that we were able to save Gemma and hundreds of other dogs and cats just like her."

Customer as Hero: What is your customer's goal? What do they want to do? With the customer as hero, your product allows them to do it. Guber used Under Armour as an example. "Every Under Armour product helped the customer perform like a pro. Under Armour would provide the physical assist and the emotional propulsion, but it was the customer who would break higher and higher personal records." I can't help but think about those emergency ladders that you hook to the window to escape a fire. An advertiser would likely focus on the mother, father, or babysitter that *uses* the ladder to rush a child to safety, as the hero, rather than the ladder itself.

Product as Hero: I had a car accident a few years ago. I swerved to avoid a rock coming at my windshield, lost control of the car and ended up rolling five times before landing upright (though facing the wrong direction). I sit here today with a tiny scar on my left wrist and possibly a scar on my scalp from where the busted window glass cut me. Many people have remarked that angels, or God, or some other spiritual protector was with me that day. I don't disagree with possible divine intervention, but that's not where I give the credit. A few weeks after the accident, I wrote a long letter to Toyota. I thanked them for the thousands of man-hours that went into ensuring that in case of a rollover, the cab of the vehicle would remain intact. I thanked them for making a product that ultimately saved my life and left me in the same condition (bumps, cuts, and concussion notwithstanding) as when I set out on my drive that day. Although I was the main character of that story, my Toyota Corolla was the hero that day. And while it went to that big junkyard in the sky, I'm now the proud (and safe) owner of a Toyota Camry.

Goal and Conflict

What does the MC of your story want to accomplish? And what is the conflict or whatever is standing in their way? Often, this will be a similar or even identical problem to that of your potential customer.

If you are selling investment products, perhaps your main character wanted to retire at a reasonable age. The conflict could be that they have no savings and live paycheck to paycheck.

Maybe their goal is to put their kids through college, but again, they are barely making ends meet.

Solution

Ideally, your product will help the MC overcome whatever it is that ails them.

Emotion

When you sit down to craft a story, you need to ask yourself the following questions: What do I want my audience to feel? Act? Do?

I used to belong to a critique group. I would sit down with two other writers and we would read each other's work and then lovingly tear it to shreds. We'd tear it apart so we could build it back up stronger. It was never planned this way, but we each had a role in the group. One of the women was always checking for continuity: did you skip something, repeat something, head hop (I'll explain that later), or did you have a sex scene where your main character took her shirt off four times (guilty as charged). Our token male was the "action" guy, he'd actually jump up and act out scenes to make sure that they made sense. And then there was me. I was the "emotion" police. Maybe it's my psychology background, but you could often find me leaning my chin in my hand and asking, "How did that make you feel?"

How did your character feel throughout the story? We want to share the emotional journey along with the physical journey. Did they feel hopeless? Were they frightened? The only way to put yourself in someone's shoes is to know how they feel. You may have to play therapist with yourself (totally different than playing doctor). Just keep asking "How did that make you feel," until you eventually blame your mother.

But seriously, crafting the perfect story is all about figuring out your customer's pain points and then finding an experience that supports how your product or service heals those points.

Simple, right?

CHAPTER TEN
TARANTINO IT

Hopefully, you've gotten to this point in the book and realized that:

a) Storytelling is super powerful and you must add it to your bag of tricks

and

b) It's not as difficult as you originally thought.

Now, on the off chance that you have not yet embraced point b and are currently curled in the fetal position in the corner mumbling something about Dr. Seuss and spreadsheets, allow me to put your mind at ease.

Stories don't have to be a grand creation left only to authors and bards. When you follow a simple process, you can create a powerful and impactful story with little to no time spent in the fetal position.

So stand up and brush yourself off. There is no crying in storytelling. Okay, maybe there's some, but it's a good cry.

Since my name is the color of leaves, I like to think about business stories using a tree-esque 3 part structure called SAP. I suppose you could also look at it as a sandwich. Let's pretend you are a woodpecker (they drink sap... I just looked it up). Thanks for humoring me along this ridiculous journey. So you are a sap-eating woodpecker:

Setup

Action

Payoff

The Setup is your first layer of bread (anyone else picturing Woody Woodpecker snacking on a BLT?). This gives the reader (or listener) everything they need to know about the situation. This can include the hero or main character, the setting, the backstory, the character's goal, and what is standing in the way of them achieving that goal (that's the villain). In Gemma's story in the Introduction, I shared the main character, Gemma an adorable dog whose back legs were paralyzed, and the setting, the animal shelter. It goes without saying that she wanted to get into a forever family and not die in a shelter; however, her physical disability was standing in the way of that goal.

Want to know if you've nailed the setup? Paul Smith, author of <u>Lead with a Story</u> suggests starting out the sentence with

"Once upon a time, there was..." Boom! You've just introduced your character. From there, you can tell the audience what happened to the character.

The Action is the meat in your SAP sandwich. It represents what actually happens during the story. How does the main character do battle with the villain? What problems does he or she face along the journey? And what (or who) ultimately saves the day? The only villain in Gemma's story was circumstance or maybe the P.O.S that abandoned her at the shelter (no blame is placed on the vet or shelter staff). The solution is our volunteer who swooped in and rushed Gemma off to the safety of our animal rescue. Was it your product or service that ultimately "saved the day?"

The Payoff is your last layer of bread (can woodpeckers eat carbs?). This represents not only the ending to the story, but also the lesson or call to action that the audience should take away. If you'd like to sound like a snooty French author, you can also use the term Denouement. This is when we check back in with the character to see how things are unfolding for them after achieving their goal. Think back to all those fairy tales you read as a child. How did they end?

"And they lived happily ever after." Boom. You've been denouement-ed (made that up, let's make it go viral!)

Did your main character survive the ordeal? Gemma sure did. She's now living in the lap of luxury with a loving family and her own pool. Once you've wrapped up the story with a pretty, little bow, it's time to give the lesson. Why did you tell this story? Was it useful or do you just get a kick out of hearing yourself speak? I told the story because I wanted the potential donor to know that he held the power of life and death in his wallet — though phrasing it that way may have been a bit harsh. This story's ending led directly to my call to action, asking him to part with some of his hard-earned moola so we could rescue more cuties from the shelters.

Why are you telling your story? What do you want your audience to think, feel, and do after you've shared your tale?

That's it. Not terrible, right? Three steps and you go from boring the pants off your audience/potential customer, to making a real, lasting connection that helps them solve their problem, and helps you keep a roof over your head.

Now that you've seen how easy it can be, let's dive a little bit deeper.

Did you head back into the corner? This won't be scary either. In fact, humans have been doing this since the days of Aristotle. There's a structure called Freytag's Pyramid that will help you understand the Setup, Action, and Result a little more clearly. Remember the Super Bowl ad study that I mentioned earlier on in the book? You remember, first, we were talking about commercials and then you lost me for a few minutes to a dog and horse best friend duo...

Anyway, the ads in the study that followed Freytag's Pyramid were the most successful ads. And if it's good enough for a million-dollar commercial at the Super Bowl, it's good enough for us.

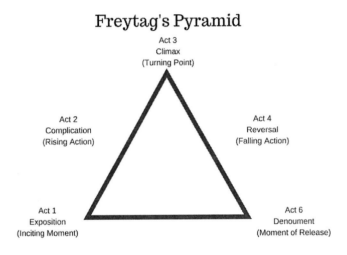

As you can see by the handy-dandy triangle, you start out with the inciting moment: What happened that draws us into the story? Then we move to the rising action: Something is making the situation worse. From there, we hit the turning point or the climax: What changes the situation? Then we've got our falling action: what happens after the turning point that affects our main character. And finally, we become stuffy French writers and show the aftereffects of the situation through denoument.

Let's head back to Gemma's story using Freytag's Pyramid:
Exposition: Gemma is abandoned at the shelter
Complication: Her disability makes her "ineligible" for adoption so she's prepped for euthanasia
Climax: A volunteer sees her and scoops her off the table
Reversal: She goes to stay with our Executive Director and gets medical treatment and oodles of love
Denouement: She lives happily ever after and goes on to win the Gold Medal in the Olympic Dog Paddle (okay that part didn't happen, but it could!).

Would you like some other structured possibilities? Karen Dietz and Lori Silverman lay out some of the variations on story structures you can use in Business Storytelling for Dummies. Take a look at the following structures and see if any strike your fancy.

"I'm Better Off"
In this type of story, the main character gets into trouble and then gets out of trouble. He or she benefits from the experience.
This is a story of struggle and redemption — of losing everything and gaining something better in return. A bankruptcy, being let go from a job, losing a home, or making major mistakes and recovering from them.

"The Cinderella Down-and-Out Story"
In this story, the MC is in a bad spot. A special helper provides gifts, but then the character loses their good

standing. Eventually, their good standing is restored, and the character is happy.

This is the most popular story in Western civilization. In business, this could be a story of dissatisfying work and living in desperation. Then a mentor comes along and transforms the person's life, but circumstances still hold the character back. These are eventually resolved which leads to the character's dreams being realized.

"SHARES"
In this story, you start with a <u>S</u>etting ("I was sitting at my desk..."), followed by the <u>H</u>indrance or obstacles that's creating the problem. The <u>A</u>ction that was taken is given next, followed by the <u>R</u>esult. The teller then proves a statement evaluating the <u>E</u>xperience ("this made me think about..."), ending with <u>S</u>uggested actions.

This is a very useful structure to use when time is limited. It's particularly helpful during interviews or in email newsletters and on blogs where space is short.

"Leverage the Underdog"
1. Describe the significant struggle that the person has experienced.
2. Insert a hint of hope.
3. Share the moment of deliverance from the struggle.
4. Provide the key message.
5. Reference back to the implied action steps or attitudes if this can be done appropriately.

6. Show how your organization is celebrating the success.

People love underdogs. Think Superman, Spiderman, and other favorite heroes who experience deliverance. Hint: We're all heroes who've experienced deliverance, and many of your customers are underdogs who have overcome and persevered. Hope is the ultimate message.

Hopefully, that got your creative juices flowing and you are feverishly scribbling story ideas in a notebook. However, it may have also left you with the all-important question: Where do I start?

The examples I've presented so far throughout this book, have shown the merits of "linear storytelling." This is the most traditional structure for a story, and likely, the one you'll use the most often. This is how the world is - this is what changes it - this is what the world becomes.

However, there is something to keep in mind. If you spend too much time getting to the "meat" of the story, the action, your audience will be left asking "Where's the beef?" Did I just majorly age myself?

Many books, movies, business stories, and barroom tales have left audiences wondering, "Are they going to get to the point soon or should I just fake a heart attack?" Please don't do that to your audience. Especially not with your business stories, as the listener doesn't have the benefit of several shots of tequila in his system.

How do we avoid this?

This technique isn't for the faint of heart... you Tarantino it.

Now, I'm fairly sure that I'm not the first person to use this legendary director as a verb, and I won't be the last, either. There's an actual screenwriting technique called "medias res" which is Latin for "into the middle of things." But I'm going to stick to calling it Tarantino-ing.

Moving on.

Like his work or not, you have to admit that Quentin Tarantino doesn't play by traditional rules. He opens his story right in the middle of the action with little to no explanation of the back story, characters, or plot of the movie. I don't think I've ever heard anyone say they were "bored" during a Tarantino flick. "Horrified," "disgusted," "morally taken aback," or "running for the bathroom," but never bored.

So the question remains, where do I start?

The answer: as close to the action as possible without leaving your audience spinning around and mumbling "who the... what the... where the...?" before collapsing into a pile of confusion and regret.

Remember that the audience connects with the character

and needs to establish emotional attachment in order to empathize and follow the hero's journey. However, also remember that we don't need to know what the main character had for lunch in elementary school - unless it plays into the challenge at hand.

I once bit into my peanut butter and jelly sandwich in the lunchroom and got a big hunk of strawberry stuck between my teeth. The embarrassment has plagued me to this day. I've got CJT — Childhood Jelly Trauma — and it has affected my grocery purchases for years. This probably isn't an important story if you are trying to sell a car, but if you are the maker of those squeezy bottles of jelly... you just struck gold. (And thank you, I've never repeated that situation again.) Give the audience what they need — no more — and they will thank you for it.

Which actually brings me to another question I'd like to address (you'd think I actually planned this): Where and when should I stop?

Here's the thing, I'm not a fan of prattling on just for the sake of making something longer. That's why, when I'm done giving you the information I plan to give you, I'm going to end the book. Not abruptly, don't worry about getting whiplash in a few pages, but you are, no doubt, a busy person and I respect your time.

Do you feel the same way about your audience? Remember, these stories are for them - not for you. Once you've communicated what they need to know... stop talking. I always laugh because, in a Toastmasters Club, the very first speech you do is called an Ice Breaker. It's just a platform to introduce yourself to the club and conquer that first, daunting experience of speaking in front of a crowd. There are generally two types of people that go into Toastmasters. The first is the person who is afraid of public speaking. The second is the person who's afraid to stop. It's very easy to tell the difference. Not because the fearful speaker is shaking, stumbling over their words, and repeatedly glancing for the Exit. No. It's because the 2nd type has zipped well past the allotted six minutes and the other club members are glancing around the room wondering if anyone brought the Vaudeville Hook. Don't be afraid to stop talking or writing. No one wants their time wasted. Typically, a business story will last for up to three minutes. If you manage to touch on all the points and necessary details in less than that, huzzah!

There you go, a fully-fed, well-sated woodpecker. Set up your story, provide the Action, and share the Payoff. Alternately, if you'd like to try your hand at the Tarantino method, Godspeed. Just promise me that you'll try it out on family, friends, and a few coworkers before you bust it out in a sales presentation.

CHAPTER ELEVEN
I CAN'T WRITE MY WAY OUT OF A PAPER BAG

My mom is an amazingly talented artist. As a child, I'd watch her paint with ease, churning out beautiful picture after beautiful picture, all the while thinking, "I just don't have what it takes to be an artist." She tried to encourage me, offering up her painting supplies and praising everything I attempted, but her raw talent was intimidating and I couldn't bring myself to create anything.

Well, a few years ago, I decided that although I'd never be as good as my mom, I still loved to paint and I was going to take a watercolor class to inspire me. We practiced our brushwork, learned how to mix colors and create realistic shadows, and learned the techniques necessary to create beautiful work.

I actually learned to be a better artist!

Now I may never be as good as my mom, but that's okay. I don't have to be the best artist, I just have to feel free to create.

The same is true for storytelling.

Writing has always come naturally to me, (don't hate me, I'm terrible at other things like car maintenance, grilling meats, and sending out birthday cards on time), so it never actually occurred to me that there were rules you could follow, established techniques that you could learn, and tips and tricks that you could use to become a better writer.

But there are. You are about to learn them. So, if you have read through this entire book thinking, "That's great, but I can't write my way out of a paper bag," help is on the way.

One thing before we get to that though. I'd like to introduce a concept called artistic liberty. This is your story and while it's important to maintain integrity (re-read the Starfish chapter if you need a refresher), it's also important to keep your story clean and easy to follow.

For example, when I first moved out to Vegas in 2008, I was mid-divorce and mid-nervous breakdown. My friend invited me to go camping up in Utah with him and his dad. I jumped at the chance and hopped in my car to meet them up in Moab. On the second day, we were hiking and we reached a point where my body just shut down. I was 5 feet from the top of a mountain and I was done. We had been hiking for hours and I was exhausted, weak, and ready to throw in the towel. My friend Steve had his hand outstretched towards me. He peered over the last ledge I needed to traverse and said, "If you don't come up here, you are going to regret it for the rest of your life."

I gathered up strength I didn't know I had, put one foot firmly on a rock and accepted my friend's hand while I scrambled over the last stretch of mountain. The view was astonishing and the feeling of accomplishment was the sweetest I had ever known.

Now, my friend's name was not actually Steve, it was Justin. Steve was his dad. But for the point of this story, you don't need to know who is who and you certainly don't need me going off on a tangent to explain the relationship.

All I'm saying is that if you maintain the integrity of the story and the emotions behind it, it's okay to take some of that artistic liberty. If the story in its complete truth is going to involve too many unnecessary characters, span too long a time period, travel to different locations that don't affect the outcome, or have details that will cause your audience's mind to wander, it's okay to leave it out.

Now, what isn't okay would be me telling you that instead of taking Steve's hand, I had clicked my heels together, said "there's no place like the top of that mountain," and levitated up there.

With that being said, we can now jump into a refresher course of everything you learned in school and then promptly forgot.

Don't be Tense about Tense

If you've never studied writing, you may not understand the different tenses, but you probably recognize when they are used wrong. That's because your eye or ear catches the mistake and makes your brain start smoking in your head. Let me give you an example (yes, I'm purposefully giving you poor writing): *A few weeks ago, I went to the store and I pick up a jar of pickles.*

Wait. What? Did your brain just do a cartoon double-take and then leak out of your ear?

You don't have to be a writer to hear there's something wrong with that sentence. I started out in past tense and switched to present tense. Pick one. Run with it.

A few weeks ago, I went to the store and picked up a jar of pickles.

or

It was a few weeks ago. I'm at the store and I pick up a jar of pickles.

Ahhhh. Now isn't that much better?

There are 3 tenses you need to be aware of:

Past (simple) tense: We played kickball at school.

Present (simple) tense: We play kickball at school.

Future (simple) tense: We will play kickball at school.

Chances are, most of your stories will be told in Past, Present, or Future Simple. Just be aware of tense when you read your stories aloud and listen for any tense switches that might cause your audience undue pain.

Point of View

The simplest way to understand Point of View (POV) is to ask "Who is my narrator?" If I was watching this story play out, whose eyes would I be seeing it through? Here are the four most common points of view, along with examples from the business world and examples of popular culture that can help you identify them.

First person:

"I had a customer that..."

In First person POV, you tell the story through your own experience and your eyes. The Blair Witch Project was shot from the point of view of one of the characters. A very shaky, nausea-inducing POV.

This POV is limiting in that you will only see the world through a specific character's eyes.

Second Person:

"You go to the store and pick up a box of cookies."

Not commonly found in literature but it could be used for sales stories. If you are trying to paint your customer as the main character and start with "Imagine this," it can be done.

Third Person:

"She walked into the restaurant and slipped on a piece of

lettuce."

In third person POV, there is a narrator telling the story about the characters. Think about Gonzo in the <u>Muppet Christmas Carol</u>.

Concrete vs Abstract Ideas

Do you remember those commercials where they asked you to save a child? First, they told you that it cost just $30 a month to feed a child. Then, they broke it down and said it was the cost of a cup of coffee daily. First, wow! This must have been a long time ago if you could buy coffee for $1 a cup. Second, this story exemplifies the difference between concrete and abstract. Abstract is just a vague statement or detail ($30 a month). Concrete is something you can picture, feel, taste, etc. (the daily cup of coffee). Concrete ideas and details will go a long way to making your stories more powerful and more memorable.

Show, Don't Tell

Remember in section one where we talked about showing your customers what you do rather than just telling them? The same goes for your individual stories. See for yourself. which is more powerful?

"I remember when I crashed my dad's car just two weeks after getting my license. He was so mad."

or

"I remember when I crashed my dad's car just two weeks

after getting my license. His face turned as red as the tomato sauce he was eating and a vein began to throb in his forehead."

In the first example, I told you that he was angry. In the second example, I showed you. So which one were you able to connect with?

I rest my case.

Sensory Experience

This goes hand-in-hand with "Show, Don't Tell." The best stories are those that draw the reader into that world. Sensory experiences (sound, touch, taste, smell, sight) help create a strong connection to your audience by engaging their physical bodies and their emotions. Remember that you are not writing a novel or a screenplay, so limit your use of sensory experiences to two per story.

Dialogue

Dialogue can be a powerful tool in any story. Take a look at the difference:

A) The child ran into the street, and his mom yelled at him to stop so he didn't get hurt.

B) The child ran into the street.

His mom yelled, "Stop! You could get hurt!'"

Both are technically correct, but using dialogue makes the

story much stronger.

<u>Active vs. Passive Voice</u>

I'll be honest, I'm not really sure why passive voice exists. See for yourself:

Active: The duck is wearing a tie.

Passive: A tie is being worn by the duck.

I don't know when or why you would have occasion to use passive voice. Then again, I also don't know when a duck would have occasion to wear a tie, so I guess it's just massive confusion all around. Just don't use passive voice, okay?

Consider these best practices, but don't let them scare you. Also, please don't let any of this prevent you from writing. I'm a huge advocate of puking out a first draft (sorry if you've got a weak stomach). Your first draft doesn't have to be pretty, it just has to be done. The magic happens during the editing process and, well, you can't edit a blank page.

You have a story, I promise. In fact, I want you to picture the scene in <u>Pretty Woman</u> where the man is leaning over the balcony screaming, "Welcome to Hollywood! What's your dream?" What he's saying now is, "Welcome to storytelling! What's your story?"

CHAPTER TWELVE
I'VE FALLEN AND I CAN'T GET UP: STORY TRAPS TO AVOID

I have a confession to make.

My name is Sheryl and I am a comma-holic. I just love them. In any given piece, my editor will have to remove 30-40% of my commas. I put them everywhere. Anywhere. Commas are my friend. And don't get me started on the ellipses. Oooooh.

We all have weak spots in our writing and storytelling. That's why editors and practice audiences exist. They are those wonderful people who mark up your work with a red pen or cock their heads to the side (like a puppy who's just been refused a seat at the dinner table), when you say something that doesn't make sense.

If you are creating a written story that will be included on your website, marketing material, in an article, anywhere that eyes will see it... you need an editor. Every great writer has an editor and you will be no exception. Your brain knows what you meant to say, and it will read it just as you intended — whether it's written that way or not. Having a second pair of eyes, whether they are paid eyes or just a trusted friend or colleague with a good knowledge of the English language, will ensure that your copy is clean and doesn't cause people (like me) to stop reading because you made a grammatical error. Trust me, there are a lot of people out there like that. Grammarly.com is a great resource. It has greatly cut down on the number of commas that my editor needs to contend with. It's not a replacement for human eyes, but it helps.

Now if you are working on an oral story, either for a group presentation or a one-on-one sales situation, you'll need to practice in front of human beings. I phrase it this way because when I'm working on a speech, I practice in my living room with a dog, three penguins, and a variety of sloths watching me. While the dog is real, she's not much when it comes to feedback. Plus, she frequently falls asleep, which I'm not sure if I should take as an insult. Before you take your story out on the open road, it's good to drive it around a parking lot for a while and see if it stalls. Toastmasters is an amazing environment for practicing and getting feedback. It also saves you money: no need to bribe your friends with pizza to come listen to your presentation.

There are a few things that you can keep an eye out for that will make editing and practicing slightly less painful (for all involved).

When you are Speaking

Be Conversational

Las Vegas is home to a large number of World Champions of Public Speaking (that's a Toastmaster contest and to win that title, you have to out-speak thousands of people). Every so often, these champions will wander into my Toastmaster club to teach and evaluate our members. On one of these occasions, I delivered a speech and then sat back to receive the compliments.

Ed Tate, the 2000 World Champion, stepped up to the front of the room and said, "Can you tell that Sheryl is a writer?"

My fellow club members nodded their heads in appreciation.

"You shouldn't be able to," he finished.

Ummm... wait... what? Where are the congratulations for a job well done?

Apparently, you shouldn't be able to tell that a speaker is a writer. We speak differently than we write (which is ironic, because I write the way I speak in conversation, but I have to beat the "presentation" out of myself when I deliver a speech). Shoot for conversational, whether you are presenting to one person or two thousand. For example, when I write about a particular experience, I say "tears rolled down my cheeks," but when I speak about it, I say, "I cried."

When you are Writing

Quotation Marks

I knew a woman through Toastmasters who would create fliers for meetings, club contests, and events. She LOVED quotation marks - to the point where they became frightening.

Please arrive on time, as "dinner" will be served promptly at 7 pm.

Ummm... I'm so scared. What is "dinner"? Is she serving us non-food items in place of edible items? Are *we* dinner? I have to assume she used a template previously used for Hannibal Lecter's dinner parties.

There are three times when it's okay to use quotation marks. When you are quoting something (duh), when you are using dialogue (more duh), and when you are using a term loosely. For example, You "walked" the dogs when you really just let them outside.

Exclamation Points

Welcome to my biggest pet peeve. I've named him Harry and he is crate trained and neutered.

Why oh why do people insist on yelling? One of my favorite mystery writers of all time uses exclamation points like tissues. Everything is exciting! That lady has a red hat! The car backfired! The duck is tap dancing! (Okay, that last one is pretty cool, so if you write about a duck that tap dances, feel free to use an exclamation point.) For the rest of your writing, relax. Exclamation points should only be used to express excitement or, in the case of dialogue, actual yelling. Writers often use it to highlight important ideas, and that's okay if you do it sparingly. I always tell my coaching clients:

When everything is important, nothing is important.

Now you know how to use exclamation points!

Whenever you Tell a Story

Grand Announcements

"Hear ye, hear ye! Please find your way to the village square. I'm about to tell you a story."

You don't need to announce when you are going to tell a story. Just tell it. I promise you that no one will raise their hand and say, "Hey! I didn't know that was coming. I need to get prepared."

Head Hopping

In the last chapter, we touched on Point of View - who is telling the story. When you are writing a full-blown manuscript, you have the freedom to switch viewpoints throughout the book. You can switch with each chapter (as long as you clearly label who is the current narrator), or divide the book into sections and switch just once or twice.

When you are writing a two to three minute story for your business, you may not take this liberty. If you switch POV in the middle of your story, your audience may feel like they are watching a tennis match between two Tasmanian devils.

Tense Changes

When you switch tenses in the middle of a story, your audience may not know what's wrong, but they will certainly know that something is wrong. Keep it simple (simple tenses) and decide from the beginning of your story whether you will tell it in past or present (or future if you are having your potential customer imagine the possibilities), and maintain that tense throughout the entire story.

Skipping the Editor or Practice Audience

Do you think that Michael Jordan just rolled out of his baby crib and started kicking butt at basketball? Do you think that The Beatles were hanging out one day and decided to do a concert to millions of screaming fans?

Not likely.

While both Michael Jordan and The Beatles have innate talent, they wouldn't be where they are today without practice.

Whether you join a group like Toastmasters or bribe your friends and family with pizza and beer, you need an audience. You'll need to practice your story until it becomes second nature (and, chances are, your friends will know it by heart as well). While it's important to work on it alone, try it out in front of people before you commit it to memory. Otherwise, you may be internalizing a story that doesn't do what is intended. That's just a waste of time.

If you write the story down and decide to skip the editor, you will risk making it less readable for the general audience and damn near impossible to get through for the writer-ly types in your audience.

Vague or Too Many Details

"There was this guy... doing this thing... with this lady... in that place."

Try as I might, I can't make a sentence without any details, NOT sound dirty. Or maybe my mind just has a vacation home in the gutter. Anyway, think about details as places for your audience to sink their teeth into and hold onto your story. As I mentioned earlier, you want to have enough details that your audience can create mental images of what you are trying to portray, but few enough details so they can fill in the story with details from their own lives. Think about staging a house when it's on the market. You want to have enough decor in the house that potential buyers can picture themselves in the home, but few enough personal effects that potential buyers don't feel like they are in *someone else's* home.

Red Herrings

If you are a fan of the mystery genre like me, you've been subjected to red herrings. This is when the author throws in extra clues that are meant to distract the reader and throw them off the scent. Necessary for mystery novels, annoying as all heck for business stories.

I once heard stories compared to hiking. Your audience starts out at the trailhead with an empty backpack. As they make their journey, you give them characters, details, challenges, etc. to put in their backpack. If done properly, your audience won't be carrying any extra weight by the time they reach the desired destination. If you give them more information than they need, they end up crawling the last few miles with a knapsack full of dead fish.

Let me give you an example in case my seafood disaster didn't sway you. I was watching the SWAT TV show a few days ago, and the team was investigating the kidnapping of the daughter of a very wealthy family. They were working alongside her bodyguard, who had been shot trying to stop the kidnapping and was now wracked with guilt.

When the kidnappers put her on the phone, she started every sentence with "They told me to say..."

My stepmom's immediate reaction was, "Wait, why does she keep repeating that?" Now that could've been a red herring. They could've left that hanging and it could've bothered all of us for the next forty minutes, but they didn't. Instead, the very next line was her bodyguard explaining that he had trained her to do this as a signal that they were listening and controlling her communication. Bye, bye fishy.

Adverbs

A friend of mine was an English major in college and loves to recount an exchange he had with a professor his first year.

"Adverbs should never be used," said the professor.

To which my friend responded, "Seriously?"

If you are a grammar nerd, you just chuckled. If you are rereading that over and over again and wondering what the joke is, you're not alone. Adverbs are words that modify verbs (action words) and they usually end in -ly. A few examples:

- The puppy snored loudly.
- The duck danced wildly. (He gets around.)
- The princess kissed the frog gently.

Stephen King talks about adverbs in his book <u>On Writing: A Memoir of the Craft.</u>

"The road to hell is paved with adverbs. Adverbs, like the passive voice, seem to have been created with the timid writer in mind."

So he's a huge fan. (Oh how I wish they would create a font to communicate sarcasm.)

Before you toss adverbs into your story all willy-nilly, ask yourself these questions:

Is the adverb necessary to the meaning of the sentence?

Is there a stronger verb you could use that would make the adverb unnecessary?

Ann Handley suggests using an adverb to, "completely change the meaning of an action, and not just augment it."

You don't get extra points for the number of words you use. The simpler, the better.

Cliches

The first time I told the story about Gemma, I described her as having a "heart of gold" and I nearly slapped myself. Yuck. Could I be any more cliche? Why don't I just say you should eat your words?

Unless you are sitting down to a nice bowl of alphabet soup, come up with something better. Cliches are lazy. Don't be lazy.

Being Weak

According to Jutkowitz, "If you're going to speak, make sure you're bullish about what you're going to say. When a storyteller is half-hearted — whether it's in a written piece, short film, speech, or any other form of communication— it's obvious to the audience and, thereby, far less compelling. As the adage goes, say what you mean and mean what you say; otherwise, no one will care about your message."

It's about to happen again... I'm going to make a sports reference. Hold on to your undies.

In boxing, when a fighter doesn't give it all they've got, when they hold back and hit less hard than they can, it's called "pulling punches." As someone who sprained her wrist the very first time she threw a punch, I can't say you should give it all you've got when you are fighting, but for sure, don't pull punches when you are storytelling.

Go all out. Put everything you've got into that story. Don't be wishy-washy, non-committal, or afraid to ruffle feathers. (Does that count as a cliche? I believe since it's the third reference to a duck in this book, it should be allowed.) Remember, your job is to evoke emotion and your story is the tool you use to do it.

Purple Prose

When you curl up with a good mystery, romance, or horror novel, you are looking to be transported into another world with vivid imagery, where you can practically taste the morning dew in the air. You'll happily sit through a few paragraphs of description before you get to the action because you are looking for an escape.

Your potential clients are not looking for an escape. They are looking to be told a quick tale so they can make a decision (subconsciously, of course) about whether or not they want to buy your product. They will not wait several paragraphs for you to get to the point. If they are listening to this story, you may notice their bodies go limp as they slip into a deep sleep and slide off their chairs. If they are reading the story, they'll stop.

Flowery, overly descriptive language has no place in business writing. You can paint a picture for the audience, but do it quickly and efficiently, and make sure that it supports your point.

Using Fancy Shmancy Words

Congratulations, you've finished up your Word of the Day toilet paper!

Just because you know a bunch of big words, doesn't mean that you need to use them. Your goal is to help your audience identify with your story, not alienate them because they don't understand. If you make your potential customer feel stupid, there's a good chance they won't buy from you.

Don't believe me? The New York Times is written at around a 3rd-grade reading level. The editors want the content to be accessible to the average person, so they keep it simple and easy to digest.

This is one of the reasons that it's so important to know who your audience is. If you are marketing to teenagers, you'll use different language than if your ideal customer is a college professor with a Ph.D.

<u>Horrifying the Audience</u>

In <u>Tell To Win</u>, Peter Guber talks about when Bill Haber left a company he'd co-founded and built, Creative Artist's Agency, to work with Save the Children. Bill explained that it's nearly impossible to connect with potential donors when you're trying to tell them about thirty-five million children. However, using the story of just one child, allows you to tug at their heart strings. But you can go too far; you have to walk a very fine line between emotionally connecting and emotionally destructive.

"When I came here," Bill said, "their most successful advertising was that Pulitzer Prize-winning picture of a little kid dying with the vulture over it. I told them, 'I cannot be here and have that picture. You've gone too far.' That's not the way to tell the story. You can't win people's hearts by horrifying them. Very quickly, they'll turn away to protect themselves."

This is how I feel about the SPCA ads with Sarah McLachlan. In my opinion, there are two types of people that come into contact with those ads. There are people who can stand to watch the commercial because they don't like animals and couldn't care less what's happening to them. These people certainly aren't going to donate. And then there are the animal lovers who hear the opening riff to the song and dive for the remote or bolt out of the room to avoid feeling like their heart is being ripped out and stepped on. They aren't sticking around long enough to see the website address to visit and make a donation.

However, since that commercial has been on for years, I guess there's a third group: people who bolt out of the room to avoid the commercial, and then grab their wallets and do a Google search to find out how to donate. Maybe it's effective to some degree, but I don't appreciate being horrified and your audience won't either. Find a better way to connect.

Talking Badly About Customers or Other Companies

Yes, gossip is juicy! But when you talk badly about someone, you affect your audience in a few ways:

1) They stop trusting you.

2) They wonder if the "bad experience" was due to the other party or you.

3) You leave them thinking, "If they gossip about them, what are they saying behind my back?!?"

Be careful what you say about others. It jeopardizes your relationship with your audience, and you never know when it's going to come back and bite you in the butt.

Not Knowing Where You Are Going

Excuse me while I go on a Lost rant.

Did you watch the show Lost? I did. Faithfully throughout the entire series. I watched when they crashed and were stranded on an island that got weirder and weirder by the day. I watched as they discovered a smoke monster was out to get them. I watched as polar bears showed up on a tropical island. I watched until the very last episode (which I won't give away just in case you want to watch it after I'm done complaining), and let me tell you... I was angry. J.J. Abrahams admitted in an interview that he knew where he wanted to go with the show, but he didn't quite know how he was going to get there. Gee, thanks for dragging millions of people along on a journey that you hadn't planned out. The end was unsatisfying at best, infuriating at worst. Why? Because it didn't answer half the questions that they raised during the series.

Please don't make me harbor resentment for you the way I do for J.J. Know where you are going, and how you will get there.

Rant over.

Using Corporate Buzzwords

Remember that your stories are meant to emotionally connect you to your customers, not make you sound like an obnoxious corporate jockey. To avoid this, please strikes the following words and phrases from your vocabulary:

Game changer
Open the kimono
Bandwidth
Buy-In
Cutting Edge (or Bleeding Edge)

And if I ever find out that you used the word "Synergy" in a story, I will track you down and beat you senseless.

Being Perfect

With all of this cautionary advice, it seems necessary to mention that striving for perfection will paralyze you. I'm not telling you to create garbage. The world has enough unnecessary content and poorly crafted stories. I know because I read some last night. It was terrible. It didn't make me want to do business with the "expert" who wrote it.

Do your best. Create the best content and tell the best stories you possibly can. Keep studying, keep practicing, keep editing, but most importantly, keep writing. And once you write, put it out into the world. None of the stories I mentioned in Chapter 7 will work if no one hears or reads them. If a bear poops in the woods, and he doesn't have the right kind of toilet paper, did he really even poop at all?

PART 3
WHERE TO USE YOUR STORIES

CHAPTER THIRTEEN
MILK, COOKIES, AND THREE-PIECE SUITS

"If you can find a way to use your particular medium to tell a story, do it. You are bound to be rewarded with the gift of willing attention." - Alexander Jutkowitz

If you are wondering where you should use your newfound story knowledge, the answer is everywhere. Story can be adapted to every medium, sometimes even told without words. Now I'm not suggesting that you gather your potential customers into a group, force them to sit on carpet squares, and feed them milk and cookies — although, I bet there are a ton of products out there that would benefit from that kind of sales.

Let's take a look at a few situations and some of the unique approaches you'll need to take. There are many resources out there that go into great detail regarding presentation and writing skills, and everything you need to know about social media. This isn't meant to be a complete guide, just to point out the differences between mediums and get you thinking about how you can use your stories in different arenas.

First, we need to differentiate between an oral story and a written story.

When you tell a story verbally (even just reading a book out loud), you wield more control over the audience's reaction. Think about the last time you read a book to a child. Did you get really into it? Did you change your voice to represent the different characters? Did you use your body to act out the scenes, creeping across the "stage" or pretending to climb the walls? Chances are that the more animated you were, the less the kids were wiggling in their seats. They were probably leaning forward, attention focused on the story playing out in front of them.

When you speak, you have the power of voice intonation, facial expressions, body language, and the almighty pause. This should not be confused with the Almighty Paws, which could describe a canine television evangelist collecting money for Snausages.

Anyway, you've got the power. And, when you are telling your story in person and in real-time, you also have the ability to read your audience and adjust on the fly. Your energy will influence the crowd, so use it wisely.

Verbal Mediums you may Use:

- Presentations to a group
- One-to-One sales discussions
- Video or web work
- Networking

Presentations

Pop Quiz: Let's say you've got a big presentation coming up. Should you:

A) Spend the days beforehand prepping your Power Point and adding that cool swoosh feature where the words fly in,

or

B) Craft an emotionally touching story that helps connect you and your audience?

Okay seriously, if you didn't answer B, I'm just going to cry. Please don't make me cry.

Paul Zak, would've said B. His experiments showed that:

> Character-driven stories with emotional content result in a better understanding of the key points a speaker wishes to make and enable better recall of these points weeks later. In terms of making an impact, this blows the standard PowerPoint presentation to bits. I advise business people to begin every presentation with a compelling, human-scale story. Why should customers or a person on the street care about the project you are proposing? How does it change the world or improve lives? How will people feel when it is

complete? These are the components that make information persuasive and memorable. (Why Your Brain Loves Good Storytelling)

I know people love PowerPoint - and by "people" I mean the presenters. I've never heard an audience member say, "All that presentation was missing, was a nice PowerPoint with stock photos and lots of text" — but remember, when you are presenting, selling, or serving your customer... it's not about you. It's about them. Every salesperson should have one of those rubber bracelets that says WDMCW: What Does My Customer Want? Does PowerPoint enhance your presentation by evoking further emotion from your audience members, or are you using it as a crutch to stay on track with your presentation?

I'm not sure about you, but when there is something to look at, I stop listening. I'm not saying there's no place for PowerPoint, but use it sparingly, wisely, and whenever possible, hone your stories instead of relying on a screen.

One to One Sales Discussions and Video

While they may look a lot like presentations, just with fewer people sitting in front of you. No matter which route you take, stories should appear conversational. The same goes for any videos you create. Pretend the person is on the other side of the camera and talk to them like you would if they were in front of you.

Before you head into a meeting, do your homework and learn about the industry, the company, and the person that you'll be meeting with. Please understand that "doing your homework" is not the same as "stalking." If you are creepy, you will not get the sale — but you may get a restraining order. Let me give you an example:

You find out that the person you're meeting with likes the same sports team as you or went to the same school and use it to break the ice with a story = doing your homework.

You find them on Facebook and start commenting on pictures of their children = stalking.

Networking

Networking can be a little bit different because you generally have a shorter time frame (30-60 seconds) to tell someone what you do. Not only that, but these people aren't coming to you specifically, you're just running into them somewhere. You have two options when you network:

1) Tell them who you are and what your job title is.

2) Tell them a story about someone you've recently helped that illustrates what your business does.

Now option 1 isn't all bad. Unless of course, you become a Business Card Commando. What's that, you may ask?

Two years ago, I went to a NAWBO meeting (it's for women business owners). A woman approached me, told me her name and what she did — disaster preparedness for businesses — handed me a card and then flitted off to the next victim. About 30 minutes later, she did it again. And, then, before she left, she did it again. Where should we start with how wrong this is...

- She didn't even ask for my name or what I did. This means she had no idea if I was her ideal customer... or if I spoke English.

- She returned back two more times! Which means she either has short-term memory loss due to a brain injury (I would feel really bad if that was true) or she just wasn't paying attention. There were only about 20 people in that room, so we aren't talking about a thousand-person mixer.

- She never bothered to establish an emotional connection, other than disgust and annoyance. And that is not the emotional connection we are looking for here.

I was one of the last people to leave the room that day because I was helping the speaker. Guess what was on the floor next to every single seat. Yup, her business cards. Networking fail.

It's not always this bad. Most networking interactions are actual interactions with people learning about each other, connecting over a common interest or acquaintance, and then discussing the potential for business. This isn't terrible. But could it be better?

Let's go back to our disaster preparedness example. Funny, she wasn't prepared for the networking disaster she was creating. Sorry, it had to be said.

What if she had approached people with a really quick story? What if she'd told us about a company who had no plan in place for an earthquake and employees were injured or worse? Now, I'm listening. Even though I don't have a brick and mortar business with employees, I might know someone who'd like to keep their employees safe.

Consider incorporating a story into your networking pitch. When someone asks you what you do, answer by saying, "You know when..." and then tell a story about how you solved whatever problem you set up. And please, don't be a Business Card Commando.

Written Mediums you May Use

- Websites
- Blogs
- Social Media
- Internal Communications
- Packaging and Decor
- Emails
- Catalogs
- An anthology

Websites

Let's start out with websites, as that may be the first introduction to your company that a customer has. Every page of your website has the opportunity to be told through stories. Just a quick question: Do you enjoy being talked at?

Visit your average website and that is exactly what's happening. It's boring, matter-of-fact, and completely devoid of personality. Are you? Is your company? If not, then why would you represent yourself to people that way?

Don't be afraid to have fun with your website. Be conversational. Chat with your visitors as if you are greeting them as they walk into your store because, for all intents and purposes, they are. If you are often asked the same questions over and over, why not answer them on your website? Potential customers will be impressed that you can read their mind.

Websites are a great place for stories and you can include all three types: Your Origin story, Success stories (or Failure), and Cause Marketing stories.

Share a little bit about what you do for customers, and do it through the use of story. Your home page can give a brief story about the company and how it came to be. If that doesn't fit with your design, you can always add testimonials) to your home page so that right off the bat, potential customers can follow the journeys of satisfied customers. (Videos are great if you can get them.)

If you are connected with a cause or non-profit, you'd be crazy not to promote this on your website. Warby Parker does an excellent job of not only broadcasting their cause marketing story, (they have a buy a pair, give a pair model for their eyeglasses), but also, painting the customer as the hero. Check out https://www.warbyparker.com/buy-a-pair-give-a-pair to see how they did it.

Your About Page is incredibly important as it can include the company's story and introduce the team along with their individual stories. You can even include a section for customer stories beyond quick testimonials. If you look at Airbnb's website, they have a page dedicated to "Stories from the Airbnb Community." Customers will happily tell the stories for you if you give them a place to do so. Just make sure they are satisfied customers or this method will backfire.

While it's not technically on your website, review sites like Yelp, Trip Advisor, and Angie's List exist because people love to share their experiences with others. Just the other day, I was looking for a good Mediterranean restaurant for dinner. What did I do? Look at reviews. Now I don't actually know any of these people, yet their stories influenced my decision.

When you solicit testimonials and reviews, it's your turn to teach storytelling. Ask (nicely) that your happy customer follows a template so they incorporate all the necessary elements of story. Have them do a quick introduction, state what they wanted to do or accomplish, what was standing in their way, how your product or service helped them, and how they are doing after the fact.

Quick, easy, and to the point.

When it comes to incorporating storytelling into your website (and other sites), the possibilities are endless!

Blogs

Ahhh, blogs. Many businesses believe that there's no point in writing blogs.

Couldn't. Be. More. Wrong.

Blogs give businesses the opportunity to position themselves as industry leaders, go-to experts, and THE resource for information. Blogs allow businesses to reach potential customers before the customers even know what they are looking for. Imagine if the moment you had a problem, a solution appeared as if from nowhere. This is the power of blogging. It allows you to help more people solve their pain, and isn't that why you are in business?

When done properly, a blog can improve your digital footprint and get you in front of the customers you are looking for. And as you may have guessed, they should also include stories. Including a story will help connect your reader and will help support your points so the reader can remember them long after they've closed the browser.

Don't have time to blog? Well, first off there are people out there, (like me) who work with businesses to create blogs. You don't have to have the time, you just need the foresight to know it's important. And I'll share an idea that I suggested to one of my clients. Choose one of your loyal customers, (preferably one who can write) and ask them to do a customer experience blog. I made this suggestion to a medical spa, but there are many industries where it could be used. You can either offer them free services in exchange for them sharing their experiences or just discounts depending on your financial position and the cost of your services.

The medical spa had a variety of services that most people have never tried and might be hesitant about. For example, they offered colon hydrotherapy. Not sure about you, but the idea of someone shoving a hose up there and flushing me out, scares the crap out of me (all puns intended). However, if I were to hear from an average person about their experience, and see that they survived the ordeal, I'd be more likely to try it.

Get creative with your blogs and you will not only attract new clients but, perhaps, entice existing clients into trying new services or buying new items.

<u>Social Media</u>

I don't know anyone who really *loves* social media. But, it's kind of a necessary evil at this point. The good news is that you can continue your storytelling brilliance onto Facebook, Twitter, LinkedIn, and whatever other platform pops up in the future. I won't go into details here because algorithms are constantly changing, but choose the social media platforms you want to work on and then learn the rules for those specific platforms. When it comes to social media, you must play their game or you will lose.

Oooh... I didn't mean for that to sound so ominous. Feel free to reread that last paragraph and maybe put some creepy music on in the background.

You don't need to tell an entire story in a Twitter post (but kudos if you can!). You can always use an enticing headline as your post and then link to the actual story on your website or blog.

Newsletters and Internal Communications

I'm pairing these two platforms together because, in some cases, they are the same thing just with a different audience. Whether you are addressing your customers directly, or your employees so they can address your customers, you are likely sharing the successes of the company, upcoming events, and stories of customers you've helped. Remember that everyone in your company should know and uphold the brand story, so why not share it in writing so your employees can internalize it?

Packaging and Decor

Have you ever found yourself completely engrossed in a menu or placemat? Not because they had so many delicious options to choose from, and not because it was an epic novel like The Cheesecake Factory, but because you got to learn about the family that started the company, the history behind the brand, or the company core values. Think about the yellow lab featured on the walls of Raising Cane's, the bag that your Chipotle take-out comes in, even the bottle of Dr. Bronner's Castile Soap. If your product requires a package, you might as well use the real estate. If your restaurant or store has open walls, why not decorate with the story of your business?

Have you ever eaten in Panda Express? When you walk in, your eyes will likely be drawn to the steam coming off the food before anything else. But as you adjust to the environment, you'll begin to notice the art on the walls telling you about the founder of Panda Express. You'll also notice the fresh vegetables chopped and chilling in the glass-door refrigerators. Andrew and Peggy Cherng opened the first Panda Express in 1983 and have maintained a standard of freshness since then. Their website touts:

"From our world famous Orange Chicken to our health-minded Wok Smart selection, Panda Express defines American Chinese cuisine with bold flavors and fresh ingredients. Freshly prepared. Every day."

And they uphold that statement in every restaurant. What story would you like to tell your customers, and how will you think outside the box to tell it?

I was recently hired to write a story using the menu items of a new sub shop. It now hangs on the wall of the restaurant. It may not be the story of the restaurant itself, but it's still an entertaining way to engage visitors and to give them an experience beyond your average sandwich shop.

Emails

If you've ventured into the wonderful world of autoresponders, you know that you need content to keep your potential clients engaged. What better way than to share stories of customers that you've worked with that are now where they want to be because of your product or service?

Evan Marc Katz does a fantastic job of this with his emails. Evan helps successful women find the man of their dreams. His emails are filled with stories of women who had lost hope until they worked with him and are now happily coupled because of his services. Potential clients will read these stories and instinctually think, "If it worked for X, it can work for me!"

You can even break a larger story into smaller parts and send it over a span of days or weeks. Imagine your potential customers *waiting* to see your marketing pieces.

Catalogs

If you regularly send catalogs to your customers (print or digital), you have prime space for storytelling. Have you ever looked at an Ikea catalog? Have you read an Ikea catalog cover to cover because you are mildly obsessed with the store and hoping to one day replace a broken spaghetti fork shaped like a dinosaur? Just me? Moving on.

Ikea catalogs feature stories about the designers who create their furniture and the inspiration behind their work. Even Trader Joe's has cute cartoons about their products.

An Anthology

People love to share their stories. And they love to win contests.

A few years ago, I put a call out the animal rescue

supporters for stories about animals that have impacted their lives. We called it Paws and Reflect: Tales of Tails. It not only engaged our supporters, but also gave them bragging rights for being featured in the anthology. Further, the first and second place winners got gift cards to a local book store. I can't tell you how many emails I got thanking us for giving people the opportunity to reflect on and honor fur kids that they'd loved and lost. Allow your customers to be a part of your company by sharing stories.

Do you remember the Choose your Own Adventure Books that popped up in the 80's?

You'd be reading along the narrative and you'd come to a choice. Did you want to walk through Door A or Door B? Did you want to fight the ogre or try to give him a hug? (I may be making that up). You would decide what to do and they would direct you to the appropriate page to continue the story.

What if you gave your customers that option? What if you invited them to weigh in on the decisions that your main character makes and to guide the narrative. Do you think they would be more or less invested in your business? This could work in social media, emails, blogs, the possibilities are endless.

Obviously, this list of potential outlets for your business stories is not exhaustive. It's just meant to give you an idea of the many opportunities you have every day to share your story with the world. Get creative and you will likely find thousands of ways to infuse your brand, your story, and your values into everything you do.

CHAPTER FOURTEEN
SHUT UP AND LISTEN

I bet you weren't expecting the final chapter on a book about story*telling* to be about *listening.*

Your employees, your customers, your potential customers — they are all a font of information.

Want to figure out what your potential client's pain points are so you can provide them with a solution?

Want to learn if your service is meeting the needs of your current customers so you can keep them coming back for more?

Want to know what challenges and experiences your employees have had while serving your customers?

Ask them... and listen.

A few years ago, I entered a Toastmaster's Humorous Speech contest. My speech was called "Axles, Radiators, and Demons." I believe I mentioned earlier that I'm not the best at car maintenance. Well, this ENTIRELY TRUE account of my vehicle disasters had the audience hysterical laughing — yet, I walked away with the second place trophy.

My mentor took me aside at the end of the contest to calm me down and provide a teaching moment. "Do you know why you didn't win first place?"

I mumbled something incoherent while shaking my head and sending tears flying off my face.

"You stepped on your laughs," she said. "When you say a punch line, you have to give the audience time to hear the joke, process it, and laugh. If you don't give them time to laugh, they'll never laugh at your jokes again."

Have you ever had someone ask you a question and then not give you the space or the opportunity to answer? It's infuriating. It basically ensures that you won't attempt to answer that or any future questions. Don't step on your answers or no one will bother answering you.

Success is not created in a vacuum. You need information, feedback, personal experiences, and input from those around you. They will give you the content you need to craft amazing stories and create the emotional connection you're looking for.

CONCLUSION

We are approaching the end of our journey. It is my wish that you now understand how truly powerful a tool storytelling is, and that you feel comfortable enough with the process to start creating your own. I'd like to leave you with a few thoughts:

- Whether Voltaire or Stan Lee first said it, "With great power comes great responsibility." When you master the art of story in your business, you take on a great responsibility to the people you serve. Please use your powers of storytelling for good. Tell the truth, always keep your customer's pain at the forefront of your mind, and use stories to relate to them so that you can help them.
- You are always serving the customer. Your products, services, and stories are about them... not about you.
- Go above and beyond for your customers. Simply doing a good job is no longer enough.

- Be true to your values and to the story you put forth.
- "Either you're going to tell stories that spread, or you will become irrelevant." - Seth Godin

If you have any questions or could use some personalized assistance, please email me at sheryl@sherylgreenspeaks.com and let's see how we can work together.

I now dub thee a storyteller! Go forth, share your story with the world and help your business live happily ever after.

The End

REFERENCES

Cron, Lisa. *Wired for Story*, New York, Ten Speed Press, 2012

Dietz, Karen and Lori L. Silverman. *Business Storytelling For Dummies*, New Jersey, John Wiley & Sons Inc, 2014

Godin, Seth. *All Marketers are Liars,* New York, Penguin Group, 2012

Gottschall, Jonathan. *The Storytelling Animal,* New York, Houghton Mifflin Harcourt Publishing, 2012

Guber, Peter. *Tell to Win*, New York, Crown Business, 2010

Hague, Michael. *Storytelling Made Easy,* Oceanside, Indie Books International, 2017

Handley, Ann. *Everybody Writes*, New Jersey: John Wiley & Sons, Inc., 2014

Heath, Chip and Dan Heath. *Made to Stick,* New York, Random House, 2007

Huffington, Arianna. *Thrive,* New York, Harmony Books, 2014

Jutkowitz, Alexander. *The Strategic Storyteller,* Hoboken, John Wiley & Sons, Inc. 2017

King, Stephen. *On Writing: A Memoir of the Craft,* New York, Scribner, 2010

Smith, Paul. *Lead with a Story,* New York, American Management Association, 2012

http://www.conecomm.com/research-blog/2017-csr-study - 2017 Cone Communications CSR Study

https://www.nielsen.com/content/dam/nielsenglobal/dk/docs/global-sustainability-report-oct-2015.pdf - The Nielsen Global Survey of Corporate Social Responsibility and Sustainability

https://searchengineland.com/study-72-of-consumers-trust-online-reviews-as-much-as-personal-recommendations-114152

https://hbr.org/2014/10/why-your-brain-loves-good-storytelling

http://www.dummies.com/careers/business-communication/business-storytelling-for-dummies-cheat-sheet

http://mag.ispo.com/2015/01/90-percent-of-all-purchasing-decisions-are-made-subconsciously

https://hbr.org/2014/10/why-your-brain-loves-good-storytelling

https://hub.jhu.edu/2014/01/31/super-bowl-ads

https://www.spring.org.uk/2014/02/how-many-basic-emotions-are-there-fewer-than-was-previously-thought.php

https://www.freshbooks.com/blog/5-non-icky-ways-to-ask-for-testimonials

https://lorirtaylor.com/72-questions-to-help-you-dig-deep-in-telling-your-brands-story

ABOUT THE AUTHOR

Sheryl Green is a New York native living and thawing in Las Vegas since 2008. She has always enjoyed writing, however it wasn't until a divorce shook her world, that she discovered the power of story.

Having penned three novels (comedic mysteries about serial killers), she now brings her penchant for storytelling to non-fiction and content writing, working with businesses and individuals who want to position themselves as experts in their field. Sheryl leverages the power of story through book coaching and ghostwriting, blogging, website content, and speaking engagements. Her clients include two World Champions of Public Speaking, speakers, coaches, and leaders in a variety of industries.

Sheryl holds a Master's Degree in Psychology and has worked in Customer Service, Sales, Public Relations, Education, and the Non-Profit world. A passionate animal advocate, she serves as the Director of Communications and Cuddling for Hearts Alive Village and is the founder of Paw it Forward Las Vegas, an annual community event designed to inspire people to get involved and support animal rescue, and to be a voice for those who cannot speak.

Sheryl brings a unique blend of experieFnce and insight to her audiences. A high content speaker who is motivational in style, she will entertain your audience with humor and heart.

In her spare time, she likes to read, travel, hike with her Beagle/Lab mix Akasha, and do yoga (also sometimes involving Akasha).

For more information on how to utilize storytelling in your business or to hire Sheryl for your next event, visit www.sherylgreenspeaks.com or email sheryl@sherylgreenspeaks.com